FAMILY PRAYERS

SCRIPTURE UNION

FAMILY PRAYERS

by
Mary Batchelor
Beryl Bye
Michael Boultbee
Jill Dunkerley
Margaret Warde
Jeanne Wesson

SCRIPTURE UNION
47 Marylebone Lane
London, W1M 6AX

© 1977 Scripture Union

First published 1977

ISBN 0 85421 526 3

Printed and bound in Great Britain by
Hazell Watson & Viney Ltd, Aylesbury, Bucks

INTRODUCTION

Looked at from any point of view the Bible is an amazing book. When it was first written and read by families the world was very different. We might wonder how books written before cars or aeroplanes, television or newspapers could be any use to us today. And yet we know that they can. As we read about Joseph and his brothers we recognize the sort of situation that sometimes occurs in our own families. We can understand how Daniel felt when he was laughed at for worshipping God because we go through similar experiences. And as we hear about Jesus helping the people He met we feel encouraged to know that He can meet our needs, which are often so similar. As we read the Bible we all find ourselves involved because it was written for people just like ourselves. Through it God speaks to us as He spoke to them.

All the writers of Family Prayers are well-known from previous years. All are in touch with family-life, and are well-equipped to help us get to grips with the message of the Bible today. Each family is unique and so we will all use Family Prayers a little differently. Some will read it in the morning; others in the evening. Some will be able to spend more time than others. Each will apply the content in a varied way to their own situation. This is right and sensible – but the most important thing is that together you discover how relevant God's Word is to your family.

The Lord is the stronghold of my life; of whom shall I be afraid?
(v.1, RSV).
Comment: Did your family visit any castles (or strongholds) when you were on holiday last year? People living in nearby villages used to retreat there when in danger of enemy attack. It was the place where they knew they would be safe and secure.

Are you afraid of something or someone? Perhaps of starting at a new school, going into hospital, losing your job, or of getting old? If the Lord is our 'stronghold' we can trust Him to look after us at all times and in all places.

Think spot: Going to church, praying and thinking about God are not 'just for Sundays' or when we are in trouble, but for *every day*. Which verse tells us this?

Prayer: *Dear Lord, throughout this New Year please remind us that if You are our stronghold we do not need to be afraid of anyone or anything, for we know that Your presence surrounds us like the strong walls of a castle, and will keep us safe. Amen.*

I believe that I shall see the goodness of the Lord in the land of the living (v.13, RSV).
Comment: Which members of your family are optimists and which are pessimists? An optimist always looks on the bright side; a pessimist looks on the black side. The writer of Psalm 27 was an optimist. He had the faith to believe that however black things looked at the moment he would one day 'see the goodness of the Lord in the land of the living.' Be strong, take courage, and wait for the Lord, he advised.

Think: When someone you love dearly doesn't seem to have any time for God, or you are worried about some practical matter, or you feel confused in your church life, remember this advice.

Prayer: *Dear Father God, help us to be strong, take courage, and wait for the Lord, believing that in Your time and in Your way, our problems will be solved. Amen.*

God is our refuge and strength, a very present help in trouble.
(v.1, RSV).
Comment: Today's Psalm is like a triple-decker sandwich, with quiet and peaceful lines (for the bread) sandwiched between

angry and noisy parts (for the filling). Can you sort out which is which?

Think: Family life is not always quiet and peaceful! Sometimes it is angry and noisy! That is why, like this Psalm it is good to begin and end every day with God.

Prayer: *Almighty God, every day we hear news of earthquakes and floods, war and bitterness, and unrest amongst countries and people, and we confess we often see the root causes of some of these things in our own home and family. Help us to 'Be still, and know' that You are God. Amen.*

January 4   GENESIS 37.1–4

But when his brothers saw that their father loved him more than all his brothers, they hated him (v.4, RSV).

Comment: Three things cause more trouble in families than anything else. Telling tales (v.2), favouritism (v.3), and jealousy (v.4).

Joseph ought to have known better; Israel was an old man who ought to have been wiser; and the brothers ought to have realized that it is always dangerous to 'gang up' against one person. If they had all shared their wrong feelings, and asked God to help them to overcome them, the long years of unhappiness which lay before this family could have been avoided.

Question: How much sharing of feelings goes on in your family?

Prayer: *Forgive us all, Lord, for the times when we tell tales about each other, have favourites amongst the members of our family or are jealous of one another. Help us to see the wrongness of our actions and to allow our bad feelings to be changed by Your love. We ask it in Your name. Amen.*

January 5   GENESIS 37.5–11

'Are you indeed to reign over us?' (v.8, RSV).

Comment: Do you really LIKE your form leader or head girl or boy, your boss or your minister? It is always hard to remain popular when you are 'over' or 'in charge of' other people. Remember that when you wish you had a top position.

The very worst thing you can do is to throw your weight about and remind people that you are the boss.

Joseph had only had a DREAM about his future importance but he wasn't wise enough to keep it to himself. His father wasn't very concerned about Joseph having authority over his brothers, but it was quite a different matter when Joseph dreamed

8

he was to have authority over his father and mother. We do not mind other people being ordered about as long as it's not US.

Prayer: *Lord, help us to handle our authority wisely, whether in the home, at work, or school, or in the church, so that we may be really liked and respected by those who must obey us. Amen.*

January 6   **GENESIS 37.12–24**

Reuben ... delivered him out of their hands (v.21, RSV).

Comment: 'Everybody else did it, so I couldn't stand out against them.' Is this the kind of excuse *you* produce at times when you know in your heart that you should stand firmly against unkindness, bad behaviour, or the shelving of moral principles? Reuben's action undoubtedly saved Joseph's life. He could not prevent his brothers' violent action entirely, but his calm and wise words were able to restrain them.

To think over: Does Mum calm you down when you are cross and angry? Does Dad take the heat out of nasty situations at work? Do the children make peace at school when there is a playground quarrel? Jesus said, 'Blessed are the peacemakers'. That meant Reuben. Does it mean you and me?

Prayer: *Loving Lord Jesus, help us to speak kind words and not angry ones; bring people together and not divide them; love and not hate; make peace and not war. For Your name's sake. Amen.*

January 7   **GENESIS 37.25–36**

Meanwhile the Midianites had sold him in Egypt (v.36, RSV).

Comment: I once took part in a TV programme and was amazed to see all the activity that was going on behind the scenes, whilst the viewer saw only one small part of the 'set'. If Jacob had been able to see the whole of God's plan for Joseph he would not have 'refused to be comforted' and said 'I shall go down to Sheol (or "the grave") mourning.'

Think spot: Perhaps your family is going through some kind of sorrowful or difficult experience at the moment—maybe someone you love is very ill, or an important examination has been failed, or you have to move house when you do not want to. Try to remember that God is at work behind the scenes and can see the whole of the picture.

Prayer: *Father, You know the particular difficulties that are facing our family at this present time. Help us to trust You for the best and right solution, and give us Your peace. Amen.*

'Do not interpretations belong to God?' (v.8, RSV).

Comment: Handed over to merchants, sold as a slave, betrayed by a woman, and imprisoned for something he hadn't done—poor Joseph had learned a lot of hard lessons since the days when he was his father's favourite, and spent his spare time irritating his brothers by telling them how great he was going to be. He had learned to do a menial job well and cheerfully, to know when other people were troubled and unhappy, and to give God the credit for the gifts he possessed.

We do not always enjoy the hard lessons that we have to learn in God's 'school' of life, but they are necessary if we are to become the kind of people He can use.

Family discussion: Talk together about some of the lessons you have learned from God. Are you different as a result?

Prayer: *Dear Father God, we know there are ways in which the different members of our family need to be changed before we can all be used by You. Help us to learn the lessons which You want to teach us, even though we may not always enjoy them. Amen.*

But remember me, when it is well with you (v.14, RSV).

Comment: The end of the chief butler's story was to be a happy one and Joseph asked the butler to put in a good word for him with Pharaoh when he got the chance.

When things are going well for us, how often do we think or bother about friends and acquaintances whose situations are not as happy as our own? The shy girl at school who never gets invited to parties; the young person whose engagement has been broken; the friend who is suffering a mental breakdown; the Christian worker who has had to retire through ill health.

Question: When 'all is well with you', are these people still in your family's thoughts and prayers?

Prayer: *Lord, we want to think now about the people we know who are not as happy or fortunate as we are. Please bring them to our minds and help us to do something practical that will make them feel loved and cared for. Amen.*

When the chief baker saw that the interpretation was favourable (v.16, RSV).

Comment: I hope no members of your family read the horoscope columns in your local paper? We sometimes wish that we could see what the future holds for us, but I guess we would only want to know about the good things that are going to happen to us. The baker wanted to hear the same kind of good news that Joseph had told the butler—but he was disappointed.

To think over: Psalm 25.10 (Living Bible) says, 'And when we obey him (the Lord), every path he guides us on is fragrant with his loving kindness and his truth.' We can trust the Lord Jesus to be with us as we walk the rough paths of life as well as the smooth.

Prayer: *Lord, we do not know what the future holds for us as a family, nor as individuals. Help us to be contented to live one day at a time, and to turn to You for guidance along every path. Amen.*

After two whole years, Pharaoh dreamed (v.1, RSV).

Comment: In two years' time what will the members of your family be doing? Will one have started school, or be preparing to take an exam, or be learning to ride a motor bike or drive a car, or preparing to go back to College or University?

Two years can seem a long time, especially when you are in prison for a crime you did not commit, doing the job of an unpaid jailer, your friends have forgotten about you, and your family has written you off as dead.

But two years was the right length of time to train Joseph for the important job that God had in store for him.

Something to remember: When we are eager for things to happen 'in a hurry' we need to remember that God's timing is always exactly right.

Prayer: *Dear Father God, You know that, as a family, we sometimes want to advance or delay events that are going to happen. Give us patience to wait Your timing (especially about . . .). Amen.*

Then the chief butler said to Pharaoh, 'I remember my faults today . . .' (v.9, RSV).

Comment: Have you promised to write a letter, call on a house-bound neighbour, pass on an address, pay a church visit, return something borrowed, take back overdue library books, or look out some clothes for a needy family? If so the verse at the top of today's reading may be meant for you!

'Make mention of me to Pharaoh', Joseph had begged the butler when he was released from prison, but the butler had forgotten all about it.

Think spot: Before you pray let each member of your family be quiet for a minute, and try to recall any promises they may have made but have not kept, and then ask for God's forgiveness.

Prayer: *O God of good promises, we know that You are reliable and trustworthy and will keep Your Word. We remember our faults today. Forgive us and help us to keep our promises too. Amen.*

When he had shaved himself and changed his clothes, he came in before Pharaoh (v.14, RSV).

Comment: If you want to make a good impression you will not appear in front of someone in authority with untrimmed beard, untidy hair, and dirty or rumpled clothes! If you do, they are likely to think that you are a sloppy, disorganized and inefficient person who cannot even be bothered to care for your own appearance.

Joseph was not only aiming to make a good impression on Pharaoh for his own sake; he also wanted to bring to the King's notice the God whom he now fully believed was behind all the amazing adventures that had befallen him. He saw himself as a representative of God.

Discussion point: Business firms have 'representatives'. Discuss with your family what this job involves.

Prayer: *Lord Jesus, we know that we are Your representatives on earth. Help us to care about our appearance, our speech and the way we behave, knowing that others will judge You by the impression we make. Amen.*

God has revealed to Pharaoh what he is about to do (v.25, RSV).
Comment: Joseph wanted to hammer home to Pharaoh that
God was Someone who was all-powerful, and who was really
involved and concerned with the problems of ordinary people.

God gave Joseph very clear directions as to how to deal with
the situation of plenty and famine, and it seems a pity we do not
follow a similar policy today. Instead, prosperous nations dump
into the sea, burn, or pollute surplus food, and at the same time
allow their fellow men to die of starvation when crops fail.
Joseph's plan was based on good, sound, common sense, but
Pharaoh was enormously impressed.

To think over: God-directed common sense could solve many of
the problems of a family, office, school, church, factory, government or nation today.

Prayer: *Dear Father God, give us all the gift of God-guided*
common sense, so that we may see the best solution to a problem
and be granted the wisdom and energy to carry it out. Amen.

'Can we find such a man as this, in whom is the Spirit of God?'
(v.38, RSV).
Comment: Is this what we are looking for when we choose a
C.U. Leader, Head Prefect, Minister, Church Warden, Wives'
Group Leader, Sunday School Teacher, M.P., Town Councillor,
or Prime Minister? Or do we look for someone who is popular,
easy going, and who will have our particular interests at heart?

Pharaoh was an Egyptian, not a Jew. He did not know much
about Joseph's religious beliefs, and he certainly did not practise
them himself, but he had begun to see that his nation needed a
man 'in whom is the Spirit of God' if it was to be delivered from
the many problems that lay before it.

Question: Have we started to realize this too?

Prayer: *God bless our nation, guide our rulers, give us Your power,*
that we may live cheerfully, care for each other, and be just in all
we do. Amen. (The Archbishop's Prayer)

'Why do you look at one another?' (v.1, RSV).
Comment: The effects of the famine were beginning to be felt in
Canaan, and Jacob decided to send his sons down to Egypt for

food supplies. The very sound of 'Egypt' brought back unpleasant memories to some of the brothers. They had never been quite able to put out of their minds the cruel way they had treated their brother Joseph many years before. No wonder they 'looked at one another'!

Jacob was still making the mistake of having a favourite son. With Joseph presumed dead, Benjamin, the youngest, now held first place in his father's affections.

To think over: We are wise when we learn from previous mistakes.
Prayer: *Dear God, please help us to learn from the mistakes we make. Grant that each member of our family may have his or her special place, and that both children and parents may recognize You as the overall authority, in Jesus' name. Amen.*

January 17   GENESIS 42.6–17

Joseph saw his brothers, and knew them, but he treated them like strangers (v.7, RSV).
Comment: Joseph would have found it hard to do anything else at that moment in time. When people have hurt you, and hated you, you don't forget it very easily even if you have managed to forgive them.

Joseph wondered what his brothers were like now. Were they still as hateful and cruel and hasty as they had been? Had they turned over a new leaf? He would have to find out. Notice that he didn't do the one thing it would have been so easy for him to do. He didn't get his own back, there and then, on the spot!
Question: What did Jesus Christ say about the way Christians should behave towards those who hate them (Luke 6.27 onwards)?
Prayer: *We admit that we find it very hard to love people who do not like us and who are unfriendly. Please forgive us, Lord Jesus, and help us to love them. Amen.*

January 18   GENESIS 42.18–24

'. . . we are guilty concerning our brother' (v.21, RSV).
Comment: Everything had gone reasonably well for the brothers until this point in their lives. Now it wasn't so good. This Egyptian ruler was proving difficult. He didn't believe them when they said they had a younger brother. He was making things rough for them—and they, guiltily, remembered the brother they had made things rough for. They had never quite forgotten what they had done to Joseph. It had niggled away at them. They had never been really free from a guilty conscience. They knew they

14

had done wrong, and now they thought they were being punished for it.

Something to think about: The food crisis was bringing into the open the guilty and sad feelings which each member of Jacob's family now felt. This uncomfortable time was the beginning of a period when relationships would be made right again.

Prayer: *Forgive us this day, our daily trespasses, as we forgive them who trespass against us. Amen.*

January 19   **GENESIS 42.25–28**

And Joseph gave orders to fill their bags with grain, and to replace every man's money in his sack (v.25, RSV).

Comment: Earning money for doing jobs can be a good thing, unless it results in the kind of family situation where no one lends a helping hand unless they are paid for doing so! When Gran 'tips' you for chopping some firewood, or Mum offers you ten pence for tidying the toy cupboard, try giving them a big kiss and tell them that you'll do the job just because you love them!

Joseph did not want his brothers to pay him for the grain, but as they hadn't yet recognized him they could not make out why this Egyptian Prime Minister should be treating them so generously.

Prayer: *Lord, help us to serve Thee as Thou deservest. To give and not to count the cost, to fight and not to heed the wounds, to toil and not to seek for rest, to labour, and not to ask for any reward save that of knowing that we do Thy will. Amen.*

January 20   **GENESIS 42.29–38**

When they and their father saw their bundles of money, they were dismayed (v.35, RSV).

Comment: If a neighbour presents you with a bunch of flowers, your minister invites you to tea, your teacher or boss congratulates you on your work, are you immediately suspicious and wonder what lies behind their generous gesture? Do *your* generous gestures ever have more behind them than a genuine desire to show love, friendship or encouragement? Jacob and his sons were 'dismayed' when they found that the money they had paid for the grain had been returned to them.

Reuben again tried to sort the situation out by offering to leave his two little sons as hostages for the safe return of his young brother Benjamin.

Question: Which member of your family is the peacemaking diplomat? Do you appreciate him or her?

Prayer: *Lord, we thank You for the men and women of our world, our country, our schools, offices and factories who are the peacemaking diplomats. We ask You to give them wisdom and courage. Amen.*

January 21   **GENESIS 43.1–10**

'Why did you treat me so ill as to tell the man that you had another brother?' (v.6, RSV).

Comment: Are you sometimes guilty of telling half truths when you are asked to do something that you do not want to do; or when concealing the whole truth will get you out of immediate trouble or difficulties? This is always a dangerous practice, and Israel should have known better than to think that lying would have got them out of the difficulty. Judah could see that the time had come for action, not talk. 'If we had not delayed we would now have returned twice', he said.

Question: Do you spend time talking about problems when it could be better used in taking action to solve them?

Saturday project: Discuss some family action that you have been *talking* about for some time, and decide on positive *action* this week-end.

Prayer: *Lord, help us, as a family, to speak the truth at all times, even when it may be difficult or embarrassing to do so, for Jesus' sake. Amen.*

January 22   **GENESIS 44.1–13**

Joseph said to his steward, 'Up, follow after the men; and when you overtake them, say to them, "Why have you returned evil for good?" ' (v.4, RSV).

Comment: There are at least two very different ways of looking at what Joseph did here. We could say that he was cruel and deceitful to take advantage of his high position to get even with his brothers. They had not returned evil for good—in fact they had been very careful to bring back the money they had found in their sacks on the first trip and they were anxious to avoid trouble this time. On the other hand, we could say that Joseph was only teaching them a lesson, because he meant them no harm and he never intended to keep Benjamin as a slave. It was all a test to find out whether they were still heartless and deceitful themselves. Whatever we might think, it all ended happily and the family became united as they had never been before.

Question: Do you think it can ever be right to deceive people in order to teach them a lesson?

Prayer: *O God, please show us clearly how we ought to behave towards those who have wronged us. Amen.*

January 23   GENESIS 44.14–17

'. . . but as for you, go up in peace to your father' (v.17, RSV).

Comment: When the members of a family really love one another, they all feel it when one of them is ill, unhappy or in trouble. It was no good Joseph telling his brothers, 'Only the man in whose hand the cup was found shall be my slave, but as for you go up in peace to your father.' There would be no peace for anyone in Israel's family if the youngest brother had been left behind in Egypt as a slave.

To think about: When parents quarrel, children are made unhappy. When children get bad school reports, or are involved in trouble with the police or neighbours complain, then Mum and Dad suffer too. When teenagers are a law unto themselves and are not prepared to contribute to the happiness of the family, everyone in the family is affected. As Paul reminds us in Romans 12, we are 'one body . . . and members one of another . . .'

Prayer: *Forgive us, Lord, when our behaviour brings sorrow and pain to those we love best, and make us all aware of how much our happiness depends upon one another. Amen.*

January 24   GENESIS 44.18–34

'Let your servant, I pray you, remain instead of the lad' (v.33, RSV).

Comment: Judah realized that this was no time for half truths. He told Joseph the full and complete story and threw himself upon the Prime Minister's mercy; then he offered to substitute himself for Benjamin even though he realized it might mean imprisonment and slavery.

We can learn two lessons about our relationship with the Lord Jesus from these verses. Firstly, we need to be perfectly open with God and tell Him the story of our lives if we really want to obtain forgiveness. Secondly, Jesus took upon Himself the punishment for sin that He did not deserve so that we could go free.

Prayer: *Help us to tell You all about the wrong things we have done, Lord Jesus. We thank You that You took the punishment for sin in our place when You died on the cross. Amen.*

So Joseph said to his brothers, 'Come near to me, I pray you' (v.4, RSV).

Comment: 'Come here!' or 'Come near!' often marks the beginning of restored family relationships after harsh words or a serious difference of opinion.

Do the children of your family sometimes call 'Come here', when they have been tucked up for the night and Mum or Dad is halfway down the stairs? 'Come here', says Mum or Dad when they invite you to sit on their lap and sort things out when you have been cheeky or disobedient. 'Come here', says a husband or wife when they want to 'kiss and make up'.

Question: How do you respond to this kind of invitation? If Joseph's brothers had not been prepared to listen, the end of the story would certainly not have been a happy one.

Prayer: *Dear Father God, we confess that pride and wilfulness often get in the way of true forgiveness in our family. Grant that we may all learn to accept promptly and lovingly the invitations to put wrong things right. Amen.*

'Joseph's brothers have come' (v.16, RSV).

Comment: Family happiness is catching. The wholehearted forgiveness which Joseph had extended to his brothers, and their happy reunion, resulted in waves of happiness and good feeling spreading out through the household servants until it reached Pharaoh himself, and it made the King behave in a generous and big-hearted way.

The opposite can be true too, as we saw when Joseph spoke roughly to his brothers and sent them home sad (**42.7–17**). What kind of effect do others have on you—and more important, what effect do you have on others? A friendly smile can often be the first step in this kind of chain-reaction.

Something to do: Try it on the first unlikely person you meet today.

Prayer: *Thank You, Father God, for making us members of a family where we can love and share, and where each one has a special place. May the warmth and affection of our home spread to people outside it so that they may become part of Your great family. Amen.*

'Do not quarrel on the way' (v.24, RSV).
Comment: Joseph had given all his brothers special clothes, but Benjamin had been given five different changes of clothing which marked him out as the favourite. Perhaps Joseph still remembered the special coloured coat with long sleeves which his father had given to him many years before, and which had caused jealousy between his brothers.

Perhaps he wanted to see if they had really learned their lesson about the dangers of being jealous. His warning, 'Do not quarrel on the way', was a gentle reminder.
Question: How often are the children in our family sent off to school, or the shops, or the swimming baths with the same warning? Do they take note of it?
Prayer: *Dear Father God, help us really to rejoice in the success and prosperity of our relations and friends, and save us from the sins of jealousy and resentment, for Jesus' sake. Amen.*

And Jacob blessed Pharaoh, and went out from the presence of Pharaoh (v.10, RSV).
Comment: Old age was greatly respected in Jacob's day. Pharaoh honoured Jacob by allowing Joseph to present his father to him (vs. 7–10).

Old people are not usually treated in this way in our present society. Their opinions are seldom asked for, and their advice is often tossed aside as not worth considering. How do you treat your Gran or Grandad? We all grow old and one day even the boys and girls in our family will probably be grandparents.
Think spot: The way you treat the older members of your family will, without doubt, influence the way that you, in turn, are treated. Does that thought fill you with comfort or dismay?
Prayer: *Father God, we pray for the older members of our family. Help us to treat them with dignity and respect, so that they feel that they are still useful and valuable members of the community. Amen.*

'We with our land will be slaves to Pharaoh' (v.19, RSV).
Comment: Joseph, the Israelite Prime Minister, struck a hard bargain with the starving Egyptian people. Many years later the

Egyptians were to drive a similar hard bargain with the Israelites, making them slaves and forcing them to work for long hours for very little wages.

If we fail to deal generously with people, how can we expect them to deal generously with us? If Dad makes a fuss when the boy next door breaks his greenhouse window, how will that neighbour react when your dog scratches up his prize dahlia!

Sunday project: Is there someone who has behaved unfairly to your family? Can you think of a way to be loving and kind in return?

Prayer: *Lord, we confess that we do not feel kindly disposed towards people who treat us unfairly and harshly. Give us Your spirit of forgiveness and generosity, so that we can return good for evil. Amen.*

January 30   **GENESIS 47.20–28**

'You have saved our lives' (v.25, RSV).

Comment: A fifth for Pharaoh, four fifths for themselves. This was the amount that the Egyptians were asked to give to the King. He had saved their lives and it was worth it to them.

It depends how much value we put on a thing as to how much we are willing to give for it. Jesus valued us so highly that He gave Himself for us. He offers forgiveness and power here on earth and then everlasting life when we die. Some people don't think this offer is worth considering. Others see that God has saved them through the sacrifice that Jesus made and value it so much that they are willing to give the control of their lives to Him.

Question: In what ways can we give to God to show our gratitude?

Prayer: *Lord Jesus, You have given us the free gift of forgiveness and everlasting life. You have saved our lives. Help us to understand what this means and give ourselves to You whole-heartedly. Amen.*

January 31   **GENESIS 50.15–21**

'You meant evil against me; but God meant it for good' (v.20, RSV).

Comment: Joseph's brothers hadn't learnt their lesson. They brought a rather touching 'dying message' from their old father Jacob which they had made up to try and save their skins. But they need not have tried to deceive again because Joseph had no intention of taking revenge against his brothers. 'You meant evil . . . but God meant it for good,' he said.

God watches over His children so that although people may try to do evil things against us, their actions can finally result in our good.

Kevin didn't like being bullied at school, but it helped him to understand how Terry felt when it happened to him and they became best friends.

Think spot: God always wants the best for us. He is in control.

Prayer: *Lord God, we often find things happening to us that we would not choose, but we thank You that You can use them for our good. Amen.*

If Joseph was one of the great men of the Old Testament, the apostle Paul was one of the important characters of the New Testament times. For the next nine days we have readings from one of his letters—the second letter to the Corinthians. As you read you will notice how well he understood them. After that we shall read Proverbs—a collection of wise sayings, many of them belonging to the great King Solomon.

February 1   **2 CORINTHIANS 1.3–7**

What a wonderful God we have . . . the one who so wonderfully comforts and strengthens us in all our hardships and trials (vs.3,4, Living Bible).

Comment: What is God like? If you were to go out into the street and ask people, you would get some very different answers.

One man might think God was like a policeman with a speed trap, waiting to catch him out. Another might think He was out to punish people, or stop them having fun. Some would think that God doesn't bother about people at all.

They would all be wrong. Look at today's verse which tells us what God is really like.

Question: What do your friends think God is like? If we learn today's verse by heart we shall be able to tell them what He is really like when the chance comes.

Prayer: *Thank You, Father, for caring about us, especially when we are going through hard times. You are wonderful! Amen.*

February 2   **2 CORINTHIANS 5.16–19**

God was in Christ, restoring the world to himself, no longer counting men's sins against them but blotting them out (v.19, Living Bible).

Comment: Roger came home from school with a bad report. If

21

only he could tear it up; or blot out the words: 'Lazy, dis-obedient . . .'

Mum had planned an evening out with a friend. Dad forgot he'd promised to be home early; so Mum flew at him when he came in late, saying all the worst things she could say about men. If only she could take back those words which had hurt.

Jane was jealous of her sister having a boy friend; so she told tales and made trouble to break up the friendship. When she saw how unhappy her sister was, Jane wished she could wipe out the trouble she'd made.

Question: Does God want to count our sins against us? Can He do anything about our sins and failures?

Prayer: *Your Word tells us that if we confess our sins and ask You to forgive us, Lord, You are willing to blot them out and forget them. Help us to believe this and act upon it. Amen.*

February 3   2 CORINTHIANS 5.20–21 and 6.1–12

God took the sinless Christ and poured into Him our sins. Then, in exchange, he poured God's goodness into us! (v.21, Living Bible).
Comment: Think back to yesterday: Roger can't really tear up his bad report and forget about it. Mum can't take back those spiteful words. Jane can't pretend that the quarrel never happened. We can't blot out the past, however much we are sorry. And what about the future? If Roger is lazy, he will always get bad reports. If Mum is bad tempered, she will keep on hurting people. If Jane is jealous, she'll always be making trouble. We can't change ourselves, however hard we try. But God can! God can blot out the past, and pour it away, like dirty water out of a bottle. God can change us and give us a new, clean way of life if we really want it —like clean, fresh water poured into an empty bottle.
Keynote: 1 John 1.7.
Prayer: *Heavenly Father, there are so many things that need changing in our lives. Pour Your goodness into us so that we become more like Jesus day by day, for His sake. Amen.*

February 4   2 CORINTHIANS 6.3–10

We stand true to the Lord whether others honour us or despise us, whether they criticize us or commend us (v.8, Living Bible).
Comment: What would you call a soldier who changes sides when the battle is going against him?

What would you call a spy who gives away secrets to the enemy?

What would you call a friend who lets you down when the others are against you?

Christians are God's soldiers. However small God's army seems, they must keep fighting for Him.

Christians are God's spies. They must beware of bribes and promises from an enemy who is trying to catch them.

Christians are God's friends, however much they may be teased or despised for following Him.

Prayer: *Lord, You know there are people who think us silly to obey You and believe the Bible. Please help us to see that we are safe when we stand true to You. Amen.*

February 5   2 CORINTHIANS 8.1–5,9

They have mixed their wonderful joy with their deep poverty, and the result has been an overflow of giving to others (v.2, Living Bible).

Comment: 'I forgot to put in the egg,' wailed Sue, as she took out of the oven a dish of what should have been Yorkshire pudding. How horrible it looked—just a thin, hard crust; and Sue had hoped for a huge, fluffy pudding to feed six hungry people.

'They mixed in wonderful joy . . . and the result has been an overflow of giving to others.' Those Christians in Macedonia were very poor; but when they mixed joy with their poverty, they found they had plenty to give to other people.

Think spot: Few of us are rich, or clever, or charming. We may feel we have little to give. But if we mix joy with our poverty, we shall have something to give to others.

Prayer: *Please give us plenty of joy to mix in, dear Lord. Amen.*

February 6   2 CORINTHIANS 9.6–10

God loves a cheerful giver (v.7, RSV).

Comment: Little Brenda wanted to give a toy when a toy service was held at her church. It took her a long time to choose which one to give. During the service she began to cry and the teacher had to give the toy back again because Brenda couldn't bear to part with it. She certainly wasn't a 'cheerful giver'.

Whatever we give to others, if we have any feeling of reluctance at parting with it, or if we are giving because someone else pushes us into it, we are not giving in the way that pleases God. This also applies when we are giving to God.

To think about: There are lots of ways of giving. They include love, time, help and even ourselves as well as our possessions. How cheerfully do we give in all these ways?

23

Prayer: *Lord Jesus, You gave Yourself willingly and whole-heartedly for us. Teach us to be cheerful givers for Your sake. Amen.*

February 7   **2 CORINTHIANS 9.11–15**

Thank God for his Son—his gift too wonderful for words (v.15, Living Bible).

Comment: Suppose someone had given you their most precious treasure; a gift so wonderful that you could never begin to pay it back. Wouldn't you want to give something in return?

God has given us His most precious treasure. It isn't a thing but a Person—His own dear Son. *Things* can be precious to us, but if we had to choose, most of us would rather part with every possession we had rather than lose our Mum or Dad, child or friend. That shows how wonderful God's love must be when He did not keep His only Son to Himself, but freely gave Him to die for us.

Keynote: Too wonderful for words.

Prayer: *We can never repay You for all that You have done for us, Lord Jesus. We simply thank You and pray that we may enjoy belonging to You and serving You each day. Amen.*

February 8   **2 CORINTHIANS 11.23–29**

I have faced grave dangers from mobs in the cities and from death in the deserts and in the stormy seas (v.26, Living Bible).

Comment: Being a Christian is not just a matter of going to church for an hour each week and sitting comfortably amongst our friends. If that is all we do we may not be living a Christian life at all. Jesus warned His disciples that they would have hard times. 'If any of you wants to be My disciple,' He told them, 'you must put aside your own pleasures.'

We may not have to face things like shipwreck, robbers and beatings but we will have to put aside things like 'I want'; 'Me first' and 'My rights'. We may have to speak out against wrong even though it makes us very unpopular.

Question: Can you think of any people in the news or known to you who are facing grave dangers for standing up for what they believe to be right?

Prayer: *Make us brave, O Lord, when we face difficulties, especially when we are standing up for You. Amen.*

24

'I am with you; that is all you need. My power shows up best in weak people' (v.9, Living Bible).
Comment: *Players wanted for a football team! Only weak boys need apply.* Have you ever seen a notice like that?
Girls wanted to work in a sports centre. Best jobs will be given to weak girls. A notice like that would be crazy.

Nobody wants weak people to work for them. But Jesus does. Jesus takes special trouble over people who are not very strong, or clever, or pretty or good at games. Jesus looks out for the ones who need a lot of help and encouragement. If you are not good at anything much, then you are just the person Jesus needs to follow Him.
Think spot: Jesus said that His power shows up best in . . . what sort of people? Why do you think this is so?
Prayer: *Thank You for wanting me, Lord Jesus. Amen.*

The fear of the Lord is the beginning of knowledge (v.7, RSV).
Comment: 'Keep out'; 'No smoking'; 'Do not touch'; 'Pay here'; 'Way out'; 'Speed limit 15 miles an hour'. We get used to seeing notices like these telling us what to do and what not to do. Some people only have to see such instructions to do exactly the opposite, but the rules were not made for fun. They are for the good of us all, and life runs more satisfactorily when we obey them. The Bible is full of instructions from God. He tells us quite clearly what we should and shouldn't do. There is nothing worse than having a set of directions that do not make it clear where to begin, but God does not make that mistake. Our text is like an arrow saying, 'Start here'. We shall never get anywhere unless we begin. To 'fear' the Lord does not mean to shake in our shoes at the thought of Him but to have great respect and reverence for Him.
To think about: Because King Josiah made a good start when he was only eight years old (2 Chronicles 34.3), by the time he was eighteen he had become a wise and good man and God was able to use him (v.8).
Prayer: *O Lord, help us to begin with You today. Amen.*

Because I have called and you refused to listen, have stretched out
my hand and no one has heeded (v.24, RSV).
Comment: 'CAUTION: It is dangerous to exceed the stated dose.'
　'NO BATHING beyond this point. The currents are danger-
ous.'
　'NO SMOKING in this area. Highly inflammable material.'
　People need to have very serious warning notices if they are to
understand how dangerous a certain course of action might be.
And yet, tragedies still occur: death, drownings and terrible fires
happen because people ignore warnings.
　In our reading, Wisdom put up clear notices—'on the top
of the walls', 'at the entrance of the gates'—telling people how
to live. But no one took any notice.
　We do the very same thing with God. He wants us to live *His*
way, and it's the best way. If we choose to go our own way rather
than God's, we cannot be surprised if the result is unhappiness
and disaster. Once we have read God's notices it is no use trying
to make excuses for our disobedience.
Question: Why do you think people enjoy laughing at others?
(v.22).
Prayer: *O God, we thank You because we can know about You
through the Lord Jesus. Please help all the people we know, who
do not want Your love, and do not want to choose Your way. Amen.*

The fear of the Lord is hatred of evil (v.13, RSV).
Comment: Two days ago we discovered that knowing God is the
starting-point for obtaining real wisdom. Today we learn that to
know and obey God helps us to find out the difference between
good and evil, right and wrong. Knowing Him also helps us to
choose what is right.
　Those who are not Christians often don't worry too much
about being selfish and proud. They aren't always bothered about
unpleasant jokes or stories. And they sometimes don't think
twice about telling lies or being unkind to others.
　When we become Christians all this should change. Jesus said
that no one could serve two masters—and either we are living for
God, or we are doing the sort of things which Satan enjoys.
Which are we honestly trying to do?
Question: Do your lives show that you belong to Jesus Christ?
Prayer: *Forgive us for all the wrong things we say, and help us
today to say only those things which are true and clean and helpful.
We ask it for Jesus' sake. Amen.*

A fool despises his father's instruction, but he who heeds admonition is prudent (v.5, RSV).

Comment: Roger saw an advert on television: it was all about the exciting life in the Army and the pay looked good. Roger had left school and was an apprentice in an electrical engineering firm, but he was now determined to give it all up and join the Army. His father talked with him and pointed out that while army life was great for some, from what he knew of Roger the two wouldn't go together. Roger wouldn't listen, but he soon learned that he had made a mistake. Within a few months he had deserted and the military police were after him. He wished he had listened to his father. Learning from our parents can be a difficult thing for us, but they have usually seen enough of life to know what they are talking about, and they are concerned for our welfare. The Bible teaches us to have respect for our parents.

Thought: Those who need advice the most are often the ones who like it the least.

Prayer: *Heavenly Father, help us to listen to Your advice in the Bible and then we shall learn to take advice from our earthly parents. Amen.*

The sacrifice of the wicked is an abomination to the Lord, but the prayer of the upright is His delight (v.8, RSV).

Comment: It's very hard to get on with everybody, isn't it? Perhaps there are a few people, or even one particular person, whom you find 'difficult'. Life seems easier when we can sit next to our friends at school, work alongside the people we *like* at the office, and when we have easy-going neighbours. In the same way, we do our best to avoid the people who irritate us, because they don't seem to do things in the way that we do.... Well, whom do you prefer?

God prefers to talk with and listen to *His* friends: to the person who knows and loves Him, who is following His plan, and learning to think about things in the same way that God does. Are we friends of God, or do we make Him feel sad and uncomfortable?

Question: What makes a happy face? (v.13).

Prayer: *Lord, help us to please You today, in all that we do and think and say. Thank You that You listen to our prayers. Help us to pray in the right way, and for the right things. Amen.*

Better is a little with the fear of the Lord than great treasure and trouble with it (v.16, RSV).

Comment: I once heard over the radio an interview with a man who had just won a lot of money on the pools. He spoke as if all his troubles were now over. He was going to buy a big house and a car, and was even considering stopping work. Then another man spoke about the time when he had won a lot of money years before. He had thought that it would mean the end of all his troubles but in fact it was the start of a lot of misery. He lost good friends, was pestered by beggars, couldn't settle in his new life and longed to go back to the old days when he was an ordinary working man—but he wasn't accepted there any more either. Most people think that material possessions are all they need, but God warns us that peace and happiness are not found that way. They are found only in Him, and when we have the Lord we have the greatest treasure of all.

Question: Do we know anyone like the rich people described in James 5.1–3?

Prayer: *O Lord, deliver us from the evil that so often accompanies wealth. Amen.*

What your eyes have seen do not hastily bring into court (v.8, RSV).

Comment: It is the easiest thing in the world to criticize! We find faults in other people and criticize them because although we know that there are many faults in ourselves, we don't want others to seem nicer people than *we* are. And the reason for that is that we are too proud. The writer is warning us that if we do put ourselves forward, we shall probably be put down a peg! If we try to score a point over someone else, we shall certainly have a black mark before very long. We need to see ourselves as God sees us.

When we are tempted to talk about someone, or pass on a bit of gossip, we must ask ourselves: Is it true, or do I know only one side of the story? What good will it do? Could they say the same about me?

Question: What *should* we do when we have a disagreement or criticism of someone (v.9)?

Prayer: *Loving Father, help us to know what are the wrong things that others find in us, and show us how to put them right. Save us from criticizing and telling tales on other people. Help us to take correction and advice as eagerly as we give it. For Jesus' sake we ask it. Amen.*

If your enemy is hungry, give him bread to eat (v.21, RSV).
Comment: 'Put yourself in his shoes!' The one thing which all these verses seem to suggest is, that we need to learn a great deal more consideration for other people, and their feelings. Are you a thorough nuisance to the folk next door, constantly borrowing things, or taking up their time with your requests? Do you make remarks about them which would kill any possible friendship they might have for you? Do you let people down in a crisis? Do you thoughtlessly breeze your way through other people's difficulties, as if to say: 'What on earth are you fussing about?'—leaving them bitter and sore?

Jesus told us that we should treat other people in exactly the same way that we should like them to treat us. If, in their need, we help people who dislike us, then who knows? Maybe they will not remain enemies much longer!
Question: Why do these things matter so much?
Prayer: *Please help us today, and always, Lord Jesus, to consider other people's feelings. Help us to be kind and thoughtful, and make us a blessing. For Christ's sake. Amen.*

Every word of God proves true . . . (v.5, RSV).
Comment: You have probably seen a film or a play on television which has been 'adapted' from a book—that means it has been changed in some way. When I saw such a film recently after reading the book, I was very disappointed because the film was so different from the real story. Some of the incidents had been completely changed and a few of the characters had been left out, while others had been added, so that the film was not really true to the original story. God's Word is entirely different from that. What we read in the Bible is God's story of His dealings with men, and it is true. It doesn't hide any failings in its characters: everything that God wants us to know is included there. We can rely on His promises and be sure that our Christian life will be what God says it will be as long as we can keep to the exact message (see Matthew 5.18).
Question: Is it because we do not do as God says that we so often find our Christian lives disappointing?
Prayer: *We thank You for the Bible, Lord, and that we can rely on what You say in it. Amen.*

The lizard you can take in your hands, yet it is in kings' palaces (v.28, RSV).

Comment: Have you discovered that it is much easier to learn about something, if you can actually *see* it, or even a picture of it? God has many things that He wants us to learn, and He tells us that if we look hard at the creatures He has made, we shall find out what He wants to show us. The four things described here may seem small, weak, easily misled, or easily overcome—but they can all teach us a lesson.

Do you plan for the future, like the ants, or do you live as though life will always be happy and bright? Do you know where to go for protection, like the badgers? Have you learned the secret of 'sticking together', like the locusts? And have you found that, however small and weak you may be, yet you can be in the most important place of all—God's Kingdom and service?

Question: What can the locusts teach us about our Christian fellowship?

Prayer: *Help us, dear Father, always to be ready to learn the lessons that You want to teach us. Amen.*

The heart of her husband trusts in her (v.11, RSV).

Comment: What an important little word 'trust' is! Without it in family life there can be no true happiness. When husbands and wives lose it in each other, when children lose it in their parents, and parents in their children, the family is in real danger of collapse. This tiny part of our lives can be spoilt so easily. We can ruin it by our tongue when we talk of private things outside our family circle and fail to be loyal. We can destroy it by our behaviour in moments of rash decision and moral temptation. It's sad that we often fail to appreciate the true value of things until it's too late. God longs for us to trust Him and be faithful to Him, for He has been 'faithful unto death' to us.

Question: Can we be trusted in our human family and in God's family?

Prayer: *We give our grateful thanks to You, dear Lord, because of Your faithfulness to us. We entrust You with our lives and ask You to keep us true to You. Amen.*

A woman who fears the Lord is to be praised (v.30, RSV).
Comment: Proverbs ends as it began, talking about what real wisdom is (ch.1, v.7)—an understanding of God and reverence for Him. This woman described here was wise because she *loved God first*, and all her other kindness and hard work came from that.

Notice that she showed her wisdom and love more by *what she did* and *what she was* than by what she said. Most mothers are like that. They don't want their husbands and families to be always standing up and praising them, but they do appreciate it, and never forget it, if occasionally someone in the family does something to show how glad they are to have a mother like that!

When a woman is this kind of mother and wife and home-maker, her husband is helped by her backing (v.23), her children enjoy the comforts she provides (v.21) and others outside the family find their needs met too (v.20). A mother's job is one to be proud of.

Talking point: What is the secret of being able to 'open one's mouth with wisdom'?

Prayer: *Father, make us more grateful for home and all who make home comfortable and strong and happy, and help us to open our home to those whose homes are comfortless. For Jesus' sake. Amen.*

I said to myself . . . 'enjoy yourself' . . . then I considered all that my hands had done and . . . all was vanity (vs.1, 11, RSV).
Comment: I think this is *such* a sad story. It's about a man who had, as we say, 'tried everything' to make his life happy. Yet, as he looks back, it all seems to have been such a waste of time (v.11).

As I read verse 10, ('And whatever my eyes desired, I did not keep from them,') I couldn't help thinking what an unhappy time an afternoon at the shops can be, for some families. Do you believe that people—children or grown-ups—are *really* made happier by getting just what they want, as soon as they think they want it? Ecclesiastes, the Preacher, had tried it, and he knew differently!

Question: Does this mean that fun, ambition, and to own nice things, is necessarily wrong? If not, what *does* it mean?

Prayer: *Lord, help me to want the things that You want me to have. And to know how to find out what these are. Amen.*

For everything there is a season (v.1, RSV).
Comment: A few days ago some children in our village in Corn-
wall had a party. They were having a wonderful time—until it
was time to leave. Then how young Peter howled! He wanted the
party to go on, and on, and on. Which of course it couldn't.

I am so pleased that Ecclesiastes, the wise preacher from so
long ago, reminds us to *make time* in our lives. Time to prepare,
and time to see results (v.2b). Time for sadness, and time for fun
(v.4). Time to be quiet, or to listen to others, and a time to speak
ourselves (v.7b). An old lady once told me that these verses have
even helped her to be ready to die. Because, she says, God has
given her time for so many *other* good things; so she knows that
when God says she must die, even that must be good too.
Think: Jesus once said something lovely, to help us see why
Christians need not worry when it is time to die. Look up John
14.2.
Prayer: *Thank You, Lord, for every new day that You give to us.
Help us to use each one wisely. Amen.*

**For a dream comes with much business, and a fool's voice with
many words** (v.3. RSV).
Comment: I wonder how many of us who read these words,
especially the older ones, find they make us feel uncomfortable?
We talk so much about all the good, big, important things we are
going to do. And *God* looks on . . . and *people* look on . . . and we
even look at ourselves; and find that so much of what we *mean*
to do never happens, and what we *promise* to do, we so often
forget.
To think about: We don't *mean* to be like that, of course. It's just
that life gets so busy. Children with school and friends. Mother
with home and family. Father with business, the garden, perhaps
the car. And the little voice of Ecclesiastes, the Preacher, comes
to us from the past and says, 'But you have *meant* to do so much
for God . . .'
Prayer: *Lord, help me to promise only that which You want me to
do; and then help me not to let You down in what I promise. Amen.*

Wisdom under the sun (v.13, RSV).
Comment: Is the sun shining today? Perhaps not, yet life need never be dull, even though the sky is. Ecclesiastes, the Preacher, says, 'Look around you! How *interesting* life is; and how much it will tell us, if we will only look!'

For instance, the Preacher has noticed that *brains*, rather than sheer *speed*, often win races. Have *you* noticed that the people with the biggest muscles don't win every fight? The Preacher noticed how people often get caught up unexpectedly in troubles, rather like fish in a net, or birds in a snare (v.12). And when they do, it is sometimes the person who *seems* to be unimportant who will rescue them (vs.13–16).
Think: Some people think Jesus is unimportant. People who know say that He is the Saviour of all who put their trust in Him.
Prayer: *Things are not always what they seem, Lord, and we do need Your wisdom to help us to make the best of our lives. We put our trust in You. Amen.*

Cast your bread upon the waters (v.1, RSV).
Comment: I am sure that when the author was inspired by God to write this book, he knew *just* what he meant by this phrase. Today, we are not so sure.

What seems *likely*, however, is that it refers to the ancient trade of corn carried in sailing ships. The idea being that if men were not willing to trust their corn to the ships, or spend money for the journey, then they and others would go hungry.

In the same way, the writer seems to be saying, if *we* are not willing to trust our lives to obeying God's Word, and sharing His precious message with others, then we can hardly complain when we see trouble, rather than goodness and happiness, in the world.
Something to talk about: What might you have done *differently* last week, if you had more deeply loved God and trusted His Word?
Prayer: *Gracious Lord, we enjoy adventure in many ways, but not always for You! Help us, Your servants, to enjoy that too. Amen.*

Remember also your Creator in the days of your youth (v.1, RSV).
Comment: I wonder if you can imagine how *sad* a clergyman feels when young people 'go through' Sunday School, Pathfinders,

Children's Church—and then 'forget', or 'don't bother', to keep up the practice of worship as they get older. A minister sees the other end of the story, too. The older folk, often lonely; looking back sadly to days when they used to do this or that within the church. But then they stopped, and now they tell you it is too late.

Think spot: Of course it *isn't* too late. Jesus' words of love to one of the criminals crucified with Him proves that. 'Today you shall be with me in Paradise' (Luke 23.43). But how much easier it is to *keep up* good habits started in youth, rather than begin them again when we are old!

Prayer: *Lord, help our family not to WASTE years, but to share them together with You. Amen.*

February 28   ECCLESIASTES 12.9–14

The end of the matter; all has been heard. Fear God, and keep his commandments; for this is the whole duty of man (v.13, RSV).

Comment: Are the walls of your local school as well covered with pictures as ours are? I reckon we have some real artists-in-the-making here. What we have read in Ecclesiastes up to now has largely been what we call 'word-pictures'.

The writer of the book has been looking around him, drawing lessons from life as he sees it. But now he must end, and so he gives us a simple message to sum up all that has gone before. 'Fear God . . . keep his commandments. For nothing else you will ever do will be *half* as important as that. And God will know . . .' (v.14).

Think: When we know that *God* wants us do *one* thing, but friends encourage us to do something else, which do we choose?

Prayer: *Thank You, God, for the writer of this book, and for all he has taught us. Help us to love You, and obey You, always. Amen.*

Our Easter readings this year are taken from John's Gospel. As well as the familiar Easter story we shall read how Jesus prepared His disciples for the time when He would no longer be with them. Those chapters are especially relevant to us.

March 1   JOHN 12.1–11

'Why was this ointment not sold . . . ?' (v.5, RSV).
Comment: We all know people who can't bear to hear someone else praised and thanked, or who always have to find something to criticize.

Judas not only couldn't feel pleased that Mary had used her ointment on Jesus, but he didn't want anyone else to be pleased either. He was much more interested in the value of the ointment than in the value of people. To Judas, the ointment was wasted. To Jesus, the ointment was the outward sign of a great love. Judas will always be remembered for his meanness, but Mary will be remembered for having done a beautiful thing (see Matthew 26.10–13).

Think spot: What are the things we should avoid and the things we should copy in today's reading?

Prayer: *Help us, dear Lord, to be thankful for all the good things You do for us, and to be ready to show our love for You, no matter what it may cost us, for Your name's sake. Amen.*

March 2 JOHN 12.12–19

The crowd that had been with him when he called Lazarus out of the tomb and raised him from the dead bore witness (v.17, RSV).

Comment: If you've ever seen something very unusual happen with your very own eyes, it's hardly likely that you will keep it to yourself. In fact, you'll probably talk about nothing else for days to everyone you meet.

'Would you believe it! I was standing only a few feet away with all Jesus' friends crowding in front of me, when the tomb opened, and out stumbled the poor chap, absolutely dazed by the strong light . . .'

Because those who saw the miracle of Lazarus brought back to life again, said so to their friends, many many more people came specially to find Jesus and listen to Him for themselves.

Question: What does 'bearing witness' mean? Discuss ways of doing it.

Prayer: *Lord, help me, by what I say and do today, to show others what a wonderful Person You are. May this help them to come to know and love You too. Amen.*

March 3 JOHN 12.20–26

Now among those who went up to worship at the feast were some Greeks (v.20, RSV).

Comment: You would think that only Jewish people would be interested in the Passover Feast. But these Greeks wanted to know more about the Jewish God and how to worship Him. They had probably heard that Jesus spoke about God as His Father.

Ahmed was a boy from the Middle East. He hadn't lived in

England very long but he came into school prayers every morning. Tim was able to tell him about Jesus. He explained that Jesus had died to save us from our sins and that He came alive again and gives us power to live for Him. Tim used the opportunity to help Ahmed just as Philip and Andrew saw a wonderful chance to introduce their Greek friends to Jesus.

Think spot: Jesus used picture language to help people to understand what He was really meaning. How careful are we to make things very clear to others?

Prayer: *Lord Jesus, help me to realize that there are people around me who would like to know about You. Help me to speak to them in words they can understand. Amen.*

March 4   JOHN 12.44–50

'The Father who sent me has himself given me commandment what to say and what to speak' (v.49, RSV).

Comment: If you were given a message to take to someone else, you would be failing as a messenger if you changed the message or mixed it up so that it didn't mean what the sender intended it to mean.

The people in Jesus' day had got a mixed up idea of what God was like from teachers who had muddled the truth. Jesus had to show them how wrong they were. 'He who sees me sees him who sent me,' said Jesus. Jesus was their visual aid. He made God's message clear.

To think about: Even though we have the true message about God in the Bible, people still believe all kinds of strange things about Him. How can we help to pass on the true message? Can we be visual aids?

Prayer: *Heavenly Father, forgive us when we do not behave or speak as we should. Prevent us from spoiling Your message. Make us more like Jesus day by day so that others will see what You are really like. Amen.*

March 5   JOHN 13.1–11

'If I do not wash you, you have no part in me' (v.8, RSV).

Comment: Advertisements on TV often remind us that so-and-so's washing powder is the best to use to get our clothes clean. We are given a demonstration in the hope that we will be convinced and buy it. Seeing helps us to understand and believe.

When Jesus was having His last meal with His disciples He wanted them to learn something very important. It was all about being clean, not only on the outside of their bodies but also inside their hearts and lives. By washing their feet in a way that they *could see*, Jesus helped them to understand that He wanted to wash them in a way that they *couldn't see*.

Question: One person at that meal was not 'clean'. Who was it and what did Jesus know about him (vs.2, 11)?

Prayer: *Just as we need to wash every day to keep clean, Lord, we know that we need Your forgiveness every day to keep our hearts and lives clean. Forgive what we have been and keep us clean and useable. Amen.*

March 6   **JOHN 13.12–20**

'You also ought to wash one another's feet' (v.14, RSV).

Comment: 'Fancy old Jumbo Jones taking off his jacket and rescuing Jack from that derelict cellar when he got trapped and needed somebody to dig him out of the rubble. It was a filthy job but Mr Jones did not seem to mind!'

Of course he didn't. He was the headmaster but he realized that Jack was far more important than smart clothes and clean hands.

Jesus had shown His disciples the same truth as we saw yesterday. He was their Master but He wasn't too high and mighty to do something for them, and that is how they should behave towards one another. We never lose 'face' by doing something, however small, for somebody else.

Think spot: Can you think of some special help you can give, perhaps in your own home, that you have tried to get out of doing because you felt it was unpleasant or beneath you?

Prayer: *Help us, Lord, to learn from You about being truly humble. Make us ready to do anything that will help someone else. Amen.*

March 7   **JOHN 13.21–30**

Satan entered into him (v.27, RSV).

Comment: Jesus knew that one of His disciples was about to betray Him. He could see into their hearts and minds and He knew that Satan had taken Judas over like a captive. It is terrible to think that someone who had been living and working so closely with Jesus could possibly give Him over to His enemies. Judas had allowed the wicked whispers of Satan to grow in his heart and he had never completely given his loyalty and obedience to Jesus.

This is a warning to those of us who go to church and other

religious activities but are really living to please ourselves rather than Jesus.

Question: What was it that Satan used to get a hold on Judas? (See **12.6**; **13.29** and Matthew **26.14–16**.) What can we learn from this?

Prayer: *Help us, dear Lord Jesus, to follow You as our Master and Lord today so that Satan will not get a chance to trip us up, for Your sake. Amen.*

'**Will you lay down your life for me?**' (v.38, RSV).

Comment: 'Mummy, why can't I come with you into hospital and stay with you there?' Anna is frightened, partly because her mother has to go away for an operation and she doesn't want to let her go, and partly because she doesn't want her mother to come to any harm.

Peter was upset and anxious because Jesus was hinting once again that He would have to go away from them very soon. Surely He didn't mean that He was going to die? Peter would rather give up his own life than let that happen. It was really going to happen *the other way round;* Jesus would be laying down *His* life for Peter's sake even though He knew that Peter would pretend he never knew Jesus at all.

Question: Why did Jesus ask His friends to love one another (v.35)?

Prayer: *Lord, we find it hard to understand some of the things which happened to You. Help us to remember that You accepted them knowingly and that when* we *face hard things, You know what is best for us. Amen.*

'**No one comes to the Father, but by me**' (v.6, RSV).

Comment: 'If you will come with me, I'll show you the way.' When we are in a strange place and we are not sure which way to go, what a relief it is when someone comes along who obviously knows the way. Better still when he offers to take us to the right place to make sure we don't get lost again.

The Lord Jesus says that we can find the *way* to God through Him. There is no other way or religion that can bring us to God. Jesus is telling us the *truth* and He alone can give us God's new kind of *life*.

There is a place with God already prepared for those who will accept Jesus and His way. He wants us to be sure to get there and He promises to take us Himself.

Question: What wonderful *promises* can you find in vs. 1–3 ? God always keeps His promises.

Prayer: *Thank You, Lord, for promising to take us to be with You so that we have nothing to fear. Thank You for promising that You will never leave us nor forsake us. Amen.*

March 10   **JOHN 14.8–14**

'The Father who dwells in me does His works' (v.10, RSV).

Comment: You wouldn't expect to see an empty glove moving around in mid-air, picking things up, or moving things, would you? But put a hand inside that glove, and it can do almost anything. Now it has power to lift, hold, grip, push or whatever the person wants his hand to do.

Jesus was trying to teach Philip and the other friends that God was really living His life through Jesus. Even though He might *look* like a man on the outside, Jesus was able to think and say and do exactly what God, who was His real Father, pleased. Without God's nature and power showing through every part of His behaviour, Jesus would have been no more than any other sinful man, and then He could never have shown us what God was *really like*.

Question: What should we be able to do if we have the Holy Spirit of Jesus in *our* lives (v.12)?

Prayer: *Heavenly Father God, we thank You for sending Jesus to show us exactly what You are like; and through all His helping and healing work to show us what You long to do for us, and through us for others. Amen.*

March 11   **JOHN 14.15–24**

'You will not be left all alone; I will come back to you' (v.18, GNB).

Comment: 'Mummy's coming back very soon.' When you were very small, perhaps only a few years old, can you remember feeling panic-stricken whenever your Mum had to go out and leave you for a while? Although someone else *did* look after you, it wasn't the same, and you couldn't settle to anything until she came back again.

Jesus' friends were going to feel just the same when they suddenly couldn't *see* Jesus any more. He wanted them to know that although they couldn't see Him, He would still be there with them through the Holy Spirit. He promised to come back to help them realize that He was telling them the truth.

Action spot: Can you find verses which remind you of Easter Day and Whit Sunday (vs. 19, 20)?

Prayer: *Lord Jesus, we thank You because You are with us all the time by Your Holy Spirit, even though we cannot see You with our eyes. Help us to love You and to show it by trying to please You in everything. Amen.*

March 12
JOHN 14.25–31

'The Holy Spirit, whom the Father will send in my name, will teach you everything and make you remember all that I have told you' (v.26, GNB).

Comment: If you keep a diary I wonder how much you can remember of what has happened to you already this year without actually looking it up. Sometimes other people do and say things which jog our memories and we remember things we thought we had forgotten.

As the first Christians went around telling others about Jesus, the Holy Spirit was with them helping them to remember. He helped them to write down the teaching of Jesus as well as the miracles of healing and all that had happened to Jesus since they met Him. They also wrote down a lot of facts from before the birth of Jesus right up to His ascension so that it could be passed on even to us.

Question: Do you think that some of the words of Jesus might have been forgotten or left out? (See John 21.25.)

Prayer: *Thank You, Lord God, for Your Holy Spirit who helps us to know and understand the truth about Jesus. May we pass this truth on to others with the help of Your Holy Spirit. Amen.*

March 13
JOHN 15.1–11

'He breaks off every branch in me that does not bear fruit' (v.2, GNB).

Comment: Ask Dad, if he is a gardener, or someone you know who grows fruit trees or raspberries in his garden, and you will be told that pruning is very important. The gardener has to cut out or snap off the old hard wood and branches which had fruit on them this year so that the trees will bear fruit again next year.

Our lives are like those trees. We get busy with lots of things and make it hard for the life of Jesus to grow in our hearts and lives. A lot of what we do is like useless dead wood which needs throwing away so that we have time to learn more about Jesus and work harder for Him.

Question: What kinds of things should we cut out so that we can be more fruitful for Jesus?

Prayer: *Dear Father, we want to grow more like Jesus and be useful to You. Please show us what to cut out in our lives if there are things which are stopping us pleasing You. Amen.*

March 14   **JOHN 15.12–17**

'Love one another, just as I love you' (v.12, GNB).

Comment: 'I used to like Mandy ever so much but I can't bear her now.'

'I'd like to be friends with Bill, but he doesn't like me, so what's the point?'

'Mum doesn't love me, or she'd let me have a new bike!'

There's a lot of stupid talk about the word 'love' these days, which has nothing to do with the really deep, lasting kind which Jesus was talking about.

Some people change their likes and dislikes about others very quickly. Jesus always stays the same. Some people like only those who favour *them*, and are not interested in anyone else. Jesus loves *everybody* all the time. And some folk think that proof of love means getting something *they* want, instead of thinking what *they* can do *for* the people they love. Jesus was always thinking of the good He could do for His friends; He was going to *give* His life for them.

Question: What's the difference between a servant and a friend?

Prayer: *Dear Lord, help us to be true friends of Yours, and to love other people as You love them. Amen.*

March 15   **JOHN 16.25–33**

'Ah, now you are speaking plainly' (v.29, RSV).

Comment: Has someone ever said to you, 'Do I have to spell it out?', when they think that you are being particularly dull? Then they go on to explain what they mean in more detail and you say, 'Well, why didn't you say that in the first place?' At last the penny has dropped.

The disciples were often puzzled by the things Jesus said. Sometimes it was because they were dull, but sometimes it was because they were not quite ready for the whole truth. Jesus had to take things slowly, especially about leaving them one day to go back to His Father. Now the time had come to spell it out.

41

They had come to know more about God through Jesus and could trust Him as they did Jesus. They had taken a long time to understand how Jesus and His Father could be One. Knowing this would help them to face the difficulties that lay ahead.

Question: Why was it important for the disciples to be sure of what they believed (v.33)?

Prayer: *Thank You, Lord, for speaking plainly through Your Word. May our faith be strong as we serve You today. Amen.*

March 16   **JOHN 18.1–11**

Then Simon Peter, having a sword, drew it and struck the high priest's slave (v.10, RSV).

Comment: What do you do when you're in a tight spot? If a group of bullies at school gets you in a quiet corner, or if a prefect gives you a detention for some slight offence so that you will not be able to watch the football at the weekend, how do you react? Do you become frantic and panic or do you lash out in revenge? It is hard to take whatever comes in a calm way, isn't it?

Jesus always kept calm and was in control of Himself. Peter became desperate and struck out. Jesus showed Peter that that was not the best way of solving the problem. When God allows a thing to happen, He has a purpose in it as He had for Jesus on this occasion.

Think spot: Is it ever right to fight back (e.g. in War; or when someone else is being hurt)? Was it different for Jesus because of who He was?

Prayer: *Lord Jesus, be with us in our tight spots and show us how You want us to react for Your glory. Amen.*

March 17   **JOHN 18.12–18**

Peter stood outside at the door (v.16, RSV).

Comment: So far and no further! You're learning to swim, but you refuse to get your knees wet. You enjoy country walks, but you don't want to go through a field full of young bullocks. You don't mind watching from outside the ring but you're scared to go in and box in case you get hurt.

Peter was shocked and frightened. Everything had happened so quickly that he *forgot* he had ever said he would stay with Jesus through thick and thin. He was frightened to follow Jesus right inside in case the soldiers took him and treated him roughly in return for his cruel action to Malchus. John had to go and fetch him inside, when he realized that Peter hadn't followed Jesus *all* the way.

Talking Point: Can you think *why* it is hard to show other people that you are trying to follow Jesus?

Prayer: *Dear Lord, give us courage to follow You wherever You lead us; courage to say we belong to You; courage to say we love You and want to follow You; courage when other people laugh or mock at us. Amen.*

March 18 JOHN 18.19–27

'Is that how you answer the high priest?' (v.22, RSV).

Comment: 'Don't speak to me like that,' we say when we think that someone is being rude or bossy. They have hurt our pride and we don't like that one little bit. It is then that we are in danger of losing our control.

The officer lost his control and hit out at Jesus when he didn't like what he heard. Jesus was not hiding anything. He had taught openly for everyone to hear and He had not been arrested then. The fact that He had been captured secretly and was being questioned without a proper trial showed His captors to be in the wrong. Jesus pointed this out and tempers flared, followed by violence. Nothing was settled by that.

Question: How do we behave when we are found to be in the wrong? Bad tempers can be controlled by Jesus.

Prayer: *Lord Jesus, we cannot control ourselves. Keep us from pride, anger and violence, and help us to be brave enough to admit it when we are wrong. Amen.*

March 19 JOHN 18.28–32

'What accusation do you bring against this man?' (v.29, RSV)

Comment: People will always argue about religion, the church, Christians they know, bits from the Bible and so on, but most of them never seem to want to think seriously about Jesus Christ, or *make up their minds about Him.* They may agree that He was a good man but they don't want to be involved with Him.

Pilate had nothing against Jesus, but he found Him an embarrassment. Pilate was expected to make a decision about Jesus and he didn't want to do it. If he decided to let Jesus go, which he knew he ought to do, he would be very unpopular. If he agreed with those who accused Jesus, he would be condemning an innocent man. Do what you like, Pilate said to the Jews. I don't want to be involved.

Question: Do you know of anyone who is in this unhappy state of mind?

Prayer: *Lord Jesus, help us to be sure about You and willing to be Your followers with all that that involves. May our lives help others to commit their lives to You too. Amen.*

March 20   JOHN 18.33–40

'You say that I am a king' (v.37, RSV).

Comment: We sometimes read in the newspapers or hear on the radio about a *coup* or takeover in some country. The Army or the people may be trying to get rid of their leader. There is usually a lot of fighting and the leader either manages to escape or is killed.

Jesus was in the centre of the same kind of plot. The Jews wanted to be rid of Him but their law did not allow them to put anyone to death. Pilate was being pressed into doing the dirty deed for them. If Jesus was really king of the Jews, Pilate could condemn Him as a revolutionary leader, but somehow he sensed that there was more to Jesus than that and he was afraid. Jesus didn't deny His Kingship, but He wasn't the sort of King that Pilate was thinking of.

Think spot: 'My kingdom is not of this world' (v.36). What are the benefits of belonging to God's Kingdom?

Prayer: *Dear Lord, may we own You as King in our lives, in our home and in our work, for Your name's sake. Amen.*

March 21   JOHN 19.1–11

'We have a law . . .' (v.7, RSV).

Comment: We sometimes hear of workers trying to get rid of someone in their factory or office because that person will not go along with the time-wasting, job-skimping habits of the others. They gang up and make all kinds of false accusations against the person rather than admit that they are in the wrong. It must take a lot of courage to stand up to that sort of treatment.

It happened to Jesus. The Jewish leaders could not bear the thought that He might really be the Son of God. They had always had everything their own way until Jesus came and now their selfish pride and evil ways were being challenged. They had to get rid of Jesus somehow.

To think about: When someone shows up by their high standards, do we gang up against them or join them?

Prayer: *Help us, Heavenly Father, to join with those who are trying to uphold Your high standards. Amen.*

'If you release this man, you are not Caesar's friend' (v.12, RSV).
Comment: 'It's the last straw that breaks the camel's back', we hear people say. They mean that someone has reached their limit and they can't stand any more.

Pilate had reached 'the last straw' stage when the Jews threatened to tell tales to Caesar. He was afraid that he would lose his job, so he gave in at last and passed judgement allowing the Jews to take Jesus and kill Him under Roman law. The Jews had pressed Pilate into a tight corner and it seemed that they had won.

How strange that the Jews were preparing for their Passover Feast, remembering the time when God had saved them from the Egyptians because of the blood on their doorposts. Yet they were now going to shed the blood of the Lamb of God who had come to save them once and for all.

Think spot: Choosing wrong may get us out of a tight spot but it can never bring us peace of mind.

Prayer: *Lord, we want to be Your friend above all others. Please give us the strength to do what is right when we are pressed to do wrong, for Your name's sake. Amen.*

So they took Jesus and . . . crucified him (vs.17, 18, RSV).
Comment: The Jewish leaders, or Pharisees, were bothered only about their propaganda, and were horrified to read Pilate's grand poster, printed in three different languages saying that Jesus was the King of the Jews; the soldiers were bothered only about His possessions, and gambled for His clothes.

But Jesus, even in His agonizing pain, was more concerned for His own mother's personal tragedy, and made sure that she would be provided for by making John responsible for her care.

What a wonderful example Jesus gave us of His utterly unselfish love. Even when He knew He was going to die, He was still thinking of others.

Question: Why did the chief priests want the title changed?

Prayer: *Father Almighty, thank You for showing us Jesus' great love when He died for us. May we follow Him as our King and learn to love and care for others as He did. Amen.*

For these things took place that the scripture might be fulfilled (v.36, RSV).

Comment: When we read about the lives of important people in history, or even folk living in our own time, very often the story will be taken up with the way they lived, as babies, as grown men and women; the important things they have done, and lastly, in a few sentences right at the end of the book, where and when they died.

Strangely, the opposite is true of Jesus. There is a great deal about Jesus' divine birth and teaching, but there is even more about His death with details of what He did, what He said, and the way He died on the cross. There was something strangely familiar about the way He died. It had been written about before in the Old Testament. Jesus carried out all the prophecies to the very last detail.

Special Quiz: Today you may have time to look up Psalm 69.21; Psalm 22.16, 17; Exodus 12.46; Numbers 9.12; Zechariah 12.10. See where they fit into the reading.

Prayer: *We praise You, Heavenly Father, that when Jesus died for us on the cross, the work He came to do on earth was truly finished and completed; and that He made it possible for us to be friends with You for ever. Amen.*

March 25   **JOHN 19.38–42**

They took the body of Jesus (v.40, RSV).

Comment: All four Gospel writings mention this bit of the story. When all the other friends of Jesus had disappeared because of the terrible happenings of the day before, Joseph and Nicodemus, these two 'upper-class' and well-known wealthy men found themselves together at the foot of the cross. They both wanted to give their beloved Master a noble and worthy burial. Otherwise Jesus' body would have been thrown over the city wall like any other criminal, to rot on the rubbish heaps.

Joseph of Arimathea had built a tomb for himself when he died (Matthew 27.60) and it was here that they laid the body of Jesus. Both men had been afraid of following Jesus when He was alive (see vs. 38, 39). Now they were trying to show their loyalty, to make up for the times when they had hidden it.

Think spot: It is sad that it takes a big shock or great sadness to make some people brave enough to follow Jesus.

Prayer: *We remember today, dear Lord, all those who secretly love and honour You, but who are afraid of people knowing and treating* *them cruelly as a result. Give them Your courage and bravery to be honest, and to honour You openly, for Your glory we ask it. Amen.*

Easter Sunday   **JOHN 20.1–10**

'They have taken the Lord out of the tomb' (v.2, RSV).
Comment: The Jewish festival of the Passover was a time of great rejoicing when they specially remembered the wonderful way in which God had delivered the Israelites from their Egyptian enemies hundreds of years before.

But how could the disciples be happy when their Master lay dead in a strange tomb? They had to wait all through the Sabbath day and night before they could even visit the tomb, because of the strict rules of the Passover. What an unbelievable shock Mary must have had as she peered into an *open* tomb and found it *empty* except for the linen cloths that Joseph had provided two days before.

Keynote: John 'saw and believed' (v.8).
Prayer: *Dear Lord, we worship You today as the risen living Saviour. We rejoice that You came to deliver us all from the power of sin, and to show us a new way to live. Amen.*

March 27   **JOHN 20.11–18**

But Mary stood weeping (v.11, RSV).
Comment: Have you noticed how difficult it is to see anything at all clearly when your eyes are full of tears? At some time or other, when you were deeply disturbed or disappointed, you cried and cried and cried, and were nearly blinded by the tears of misery. So it is not at all surprising that Mary *almost* missed realizing that it was Jesus Himself and not a gardener who spoke to her. The important moment came when Jesus called Mary by her own name, and she recognized His voice. Her sorrow was immediately turned into deep joy, and she *saw* her Lord unmistakably, and knew that He was alive. That was enough for Mary. She went off straight away *to do as Jesus said*—that to her was more important than being comforted.

Question: What was Jesus trying to tell Mary and the others (v.17)?
Prayer: *Heavenly Father, thank You for giving us so much help and encouragement when things get tough. We need only to remember that You are alive and at our side, and then we can face all the difficult things. Amen.*

'Peace be with you' (v.19, RSV).
Comment: Whenever you or your family have been the victims
of, or witnesses to an accident, or some tragedy or illness, the
whole balance of your life is thrown out of gear. You cannot eat
or sleep, and the terrible thing which has happened seems to
loom like a dark shadow over everything every day.

How wonderful that the first word Jesus spoke to His friends
was *'peace'*. Now they could be glad instead of sad; happy
instead of gloomy; hopeful instead of fearful. What a change
Jesus brought when He showed them that He was alive!
Question: Do you think Thomas had a good excuse for saying
what he did (v.25)?
Prayer: *Dear Lord, be with all those today who are deeply sorrow-*
ful because they have experienced disaster, or bereavement, or
misunderstanding. Give them Your peace in their hearts and lives,
for Jesus' sake. Amen.

'Do not be faithless, but believing' (v.27, RSV).
Comment: 'Expect me to believe that a man on a motor-bike can
literally take off and zoom over a fleet of buses parked side by
side! I'll believe *that* only when I see it!' And how many of us
scorned the daring exploits of a stunt-rider like Evel Knievel
until we saw it with our own eyes, on television. We couldn't
believe the reports of other people who *had* seen it performed;
it wasn't true until we had seen it for ourselves.

Poor Thomas! He probably thought the proof that his friends
were trying to give him—that they had seen the living Lord—
was a crazy illusion, or a case of mistaken identity; that in their
grief they were just 'seeing things', and he had said so.

The Master's own words, gently reproving Thomas, swept
away any lingering doubts he may have had (vs. 27 and 28).
Question: What can we believe, and what are we promised as a
result (v.31)?
Prayer: *Father God, we thank You for sending Your Son Jesus to*
be our Saviour. Help us as we take the step of believing in Him and
trusting our whole lives to Him, that we may know without any
doubts that we have His new life in our own. Amen.

'Cast the net on the right side of the boat, and you will find some'
(v.6, RSV).
Comment: 'Caught anything yet?' is not the sort of question you
should ask a fisherman when he has been out in his boat for
several hours and has obviously got an empty 'keep net'. It
would be worse if the fisherman depended on the catch for his
living.

Peter and his friends didn't want to stay in Jerusalem now that
Jesus was no longer with them. They needed food and something
to keep them busy. But even fishing, which they thought they
knew something about, wasn't a success *until they followed Jesus'
instructions*.
Question: Why do you think Jesus allowed the disciples to catch
nothing by themselves? What can we learn from this?
Prayer: *Lord Jesus, thank You for reminding us that our work will
never be a success unless we first listen for and then follow Your
instructions. Teach us that without You we can do nothing worth-
while. Amen.*

Simon, son of John, do you love me more than these? (v.15, RSV).
Comment: Wouldn't you be amazed if you heard a friend at
school had run away from helping a teacher who had been hurt
in an accident which nearly cost him his life, instead of staying
to try and help? But you'd be even more surprised if you heard
later that the same person had been made his new prefect.

Peter was now being given a second chance to prove that he
did love Jesus. Jesus probably questioned him three times to
balance the three times that Peter denied Him. The other
disciples would always remember the 'three times over' promise
that Peter gave in return.

What a wonderful comfort to know that Jesus didn't leave
Peter in his failure, or take it out on him for having let Him down
so badly. He is just as gentle with us, too.
Question: Why do you think Jesus deliberately spoke to Peter
by his 'old' name?
Prayer: *Lord Jesus, thank You for this story, which gives us great
comfort when we know how often we let You down. Help us not to
want to take it out on our friends when they let us down. Help us to
show our love for You by caring for others today, for Your sake.
Amen.*

When Peter saw him, he said to Jesus, 'Lord, what about this man?' (v.21, RSV).

Comment: Have the younger members of your family successfully made an April Fool of anybody yet, or were you all carefully on your guard against practical jokes and outrageous lies from the moment you woke up?

Jesus wasn't trying to mislead Peter, but He was trying to suggest to him that whatever happened to John *was nothing to do with Peter*. God had a special plan for every single one of them. He could foresee that Peter would be tortured for his faith, and Peter would have to be willing to live out *his own* future. John would have to be ready for God's plan for his life. It is no good looking round at the next Christian, and comparing ourselves with him or her. The only thing that matters is that we follow Jesus ourselves.

Question: How do we find God's plan for our lives?

Prayer: *Lord, give us the obedience to follow You without questioning, and not to compare our own treatment or future with other Christians. Amen.*

In John's Gospel, Jesus said, 'If a man loves me, he will keep my word' (John 14.23). Over a thousand years before, God had given His words to Israel, that they might keep them. During the next four weeks we shall see in Exodus and Numbers how the Israelites received God's words or commandments and what they did as a result.

'I love my master, my wife, and my children' (v.5, RSV).

Comment: In Old Testament times some slaves were badly treated, but others lived in happy families and wouldn't have changed their work for anything. I wonder how you would have felt.

'I'm nothing but a slave!' How many busy mothers have said this! When we've been hard at it all day, have cooked the supper and have a stack of ironing to do, it seems the last straw when the family sit down to watch television and nobody even offers to help with the washing-up. It's so easy to feel resentful when we're worn out. On a good day, however, when everything was going well, if someone told us that our family ought to fend for themselves, we should be quite shocked. 'I work for my family because I love them,' we would say.

But what can turn bad days into good days? Have we ever said, 'Lord, if only I could serve *You*!'? Yet, if we care for our families as part of our service for God we are serving Him.

Think: Christians are slaves (or servants) of Jesus Christ—this is what the apostle Paul called himself. How will this affect the way we live?

Prayer: *Dear Master, we love You. Please help us to prove it by caring for one another. Amen.*

April 3   EXODUS 23.10–13

'That the poor of your people may eat . . . and the alien may be refreshed' (vs.11, 12, RSV).

Comment: What's the purpose of it all? We spend so much time making money, or cleaning the house, or working for exams., that we never seem to have a moment to stop and *think*, to ask ourselves what life is really about.

Every seven years, said God, the Israelites were to stop what they were doing and remember those who were worse off than themselves. The poor could roam through their fields and pick the fruit; and they could enjoy the animals they'd been too busy to notice before. As well as a holiday every seven years, they were also to have one every seven *days*. Then the animals could graze to their hearts' content, the kitchen-workers could sit out in the sun, and there would be time to make foreigners feel really welcome.

Think: If we work hard for five or six days a week, what a refreshing and *different* day Sunday ought to be! How would God like us to spend Sunday? Does the passage give us any ideas?

Prayer: *Thank You, Lord, for a wonderful world. Please help us to notice and care for those who are less fortunate than ourselves. Amen.*

April 4   EXODUS 24.3–8

'All that the Lord has spoken we will do, and we will be obedient' (v.7, RSV).

Comment: Moses not only told the people what God had said; he carefully wrote it down and read it to them as well. Yes, the people understood every word, and they made a solemn promise to obey it. Unfortunately, as we shall see later on, they didn't keep their promises.

Perhaps we have promised to obey God—at an inspiring

51

church service, for instance, or when we have been ill or frightened. Have we kept *our* promises?

Research project: Three things are necessary before we can obey God.

1. We must truly *want* to obey Him.
2. We must find out what He wants us to do by . . . .;
   and . . . .
3. We need the help of the . . . .

Look up Romans 8.26; Joshua 1.8 and John 14.15–17 and fill in the answers.

Prayer: *Dear Father, please give us a great desire to please You. Amen.*

April 5   EXODUS 24.12–18

'Come up to me on the mountain, and wait there' (v.12, RSV).

Comment: 'Just a minute—I'll come when I've finished this row.' 'Can't you see I'm busy—I must get this door painted.' Do you ever hear things like that in your family because everyone has so much to do? Moses was very busy—he had all the people of Israel to look after—but he made time to go up the mountain to speak to God.

We all live very busy lives today. We have the house to clean, the car to mend, our homework to do—and we can't miss the Youth Club on Friday night or football match on Saturday. But it's important that we have time to meet with God.

Questions: How do we meet with God? And how can we arrange our programme so that we have time to do so?

Prayer: *Thank You, Lord, for wanting to meet with us. Please help us never to allow other things to squeeze You out of our lives. Amen.*

April 6   EXODUS 25.1–9

'Let them make me a sanctuary, that I may dwell in their midst' (v.8, RSV).

Comment: Do you like colourful carpets, bright curtains, gleaming white paint and the scent of spring flowers in your garden? So does God! After all, if He hadn't *invented* colours, we couldn't enjoy them in our homes.

But what about our church? Does it need a new carpet, or a coat of paint on the notice board, or some flowers outside? Does its appearance make the passer-by think that the God of the countryside and our God are two different people?

'But,' we may ask, 'what has an attractive church to do with God being in our midst?' If He *is* very real to us, surely we shall be so glad we shall want to make His house beautiful, too!

For discussion: Read verse 2 again. How much of our money should be spent on God's house, on our own homes, on those who are living in poor housing conditions, and on starving children?

Prayer: *Lord, we don't want to be hypocrites. Show us how to love You with all our hearts. Amen.*

April 7   EXODUS 25.23–30

'The bread of the Presence . . .' (v.30, RSV).

Comment: All these verses, just to describe a *table*! How careful they had to be to get all the details and measurements exactly right, while the wood had to be of the very best quality and the gold absolutely pure! Why? What was it all about? Simply this. That table was to be a constant reminder of God Himself. Every time they saw the bread on the golden table they would remember that God was not only pure and holy, but that He was *with them*, wherever they were.

The bread and wine on the Lord's Table at the Communion service help to remind us, among other things, that the Lord Jesus is present with us.

Talking point: If God is always with us, how careful should we be about paying attention to detail? In how many different ways should Christians be better at their jobs than non-Christians?

Prayer: *Dear Lord, help us to remember that wherever we are, in the office, or the factory, at home or in the classroom, You can see us. Please help us to do our very best for You. Amen.*

April 8   EXODUS 28.1–4

'All who have ability, whom I have endowed with an able mind' (v.3, RSV).

Comment: Some were to be priests, others dressmakers. The priests had a great deal of studying to do before they could be good at their jobs, and the dressmakers had to learn from scratch how to do the difficult stitches.

Some of us have clever hands; others have quick minds. What matters is, not *which* we have, but how we use them, for God has a plan for our lives, too. Perhaps we aren't sure what this plan is, because we are still at school or serving an apprenticeship, but we *can* be sure that God has given us our gifts, and we can *practise* using them for Him.

53

Question: What different abilities do you have in your family? Can you think of ways in which they could be used in your church or community?

Prayer: *Thank You, dear Father, for all the gifts and abilities that You give to us. Please help us to know how we can use them most effectively in Your work. Amen.*

April 9 EXODUS 28.29–35

'Upon his heart' (v.29, RSV).

Comment: Aaron's heart is mentioned three times, because that's where he kept his prayer list. When all the people saw him go into the holy place, they would feel very solemn because they knew Aaron was mentioning each family to God. Perhaps they would tremble, because they knew God was holy and that Aaron would have to mention their sins.

Our High Priest, the Lord Jesus, *lives* with God. He knows all about us and our thoughts. But when Jesus talks to God about us —and the Bible says He keeps on praying for us—God doesn't see beautiful stones. He sees the scars which mean that Jesus died *for* our sins, so that we can come close to God to talk to Him ourselves.

Suggestion: Make a list of three or four people—children in your class, for instance, or colleagues at work, or families in your street. Keep the lists in your Bibles and talk to God about them every day. If everyone who reads these notes does this, think what a difference it could make to all our neighbourhoods.

Prayer: *Dear Saviour, please help us to bring our friends and neighbours into the circle of Your love. Amen.*

April 10 EXODUS 31.1–11

'I have filled him with the Spirit of God, with ability and intelligence, with knowledge and all craftsmanship . . . for work in every craft' (vs.3, 5, RSV).

Comment: We may think that only clergymen should be *filled* with God's Spirit, but these verses say nothing about the workmen becoming priests. They needed God's Spirit for their own jobs. *Everyone* needs God's Spirit, from the art lecturer at the Technical College to the charge-hand at the aircraft factory; from the carpenter to the chemist.

For the children: See who can make the longest list of the jobs mentioned in today's passage. Give them their modern names. (For instance, we would call a stone-cutter a jeweller.)

For the adults: Find the lists you made yesterday of your friends' names. Think about their jobs one by one and discuss what difference it would make to their work if they were filled with God's Spirit. What does being 'filled with God's Spirit' mean? **Prayer:** *Lord, You have called us to do a job for You. Please fill us with Your Spirit, so that we can serve You better. Amen.*

April 11   EXODUS 31.18 and 32.1–6

Then Aaron was afraid and built an altar in front of it (v.5, NEB). **Comment:** Sometimes, when we've asked God to guide us to the right job, or perhaps to the place where He wants us to live, the right job or house doesn't turn up. Well, we think, we can't wait for ever. So we take the work which offers the most money, or the house which looks most impressive. Then, when we've gone ahead with our own plans, we have a niggling fear. Were we right to rush ahead? Or should we have been more patient? So we try to crush our doubts by asking God to bless the arrangements *we've* made.

God had very personal plans for His people. Do you think He has a special plan for every member of your family? If we are not sure what this plan is, or how it fits in with His will for everyone else, how can we prepare ourselves to be ready for His service? **Prayer:** *Keep us close to You, Lord, and day by day make us more sensitive to Your will in the little things, so that we may see You leading us in what seems to be the more important decisions. Amen.*

April 12   EXODUS 32.7–14

'Remember your servants Abraham, Isaac, and Jacob. Remember the solemn promise you made to them . . . to give their descendants all that land . . .' (v.13, GNB). **Comment:** 'But, Dad, you promised . . .' Do you ever say that sort of thing in your family? Maybe you had been promised a day at the zoo or the sea-side and now Dad has to go on a business trip or the car has broken down. It may even be that he has decided that the trip is off as a punishment for something.

That's rather like what had happened here. God was going to punish the Israelites for making the calf. He had said He would destroy them all (v.9). When Moses prayed for them he reminded God of what He had promised. God always keeps His promises and so the Israelites eventually came into the promised land— although they were still punished for their sin.

To talk about: Can you think of any promises God has made

55

which might apply to your family? Should you ask Him to bring them about in your family life today?

Prayer: *Thank You, Father, for always keeping Your promises even though we may fail. Please help us to believe today that You are working out Your plans. Amen.*

April 13   **EXODUS 32.15–24**

Moses' anger burned hot (v.19, RSV).

Comment: Although the Bible says it is normally wrong to be angry, there are times when it can be right. But our reasons will need to be right—we must be concerned about God and His glory, not ourselves. Elijah felt like this when he stood in a cave and told God he was the only one left who cared about God's Word. The Lord Jesus felt like this when He came into His Father's house and saw that they had turned it into a market. He turned the tables upside down and sent the coins flying. We may feel like this when someone uses God's name like a swear word, or says the Bible isn't true. We feel like a son who has heard his father called a liar. Our desire to defend our Father shows that we very much belong to His family.

For discussion: John Wesley used to tell Christians that even when they felt this holy anger, their words should still be gentle and wise. Was Moses wrong to be angry? Should we, as Christians, behave differently to Moses?

Prayer: *Our Father, may we never be afraid to show whose side we are on, but when we stand up for You, help our words to be wise. Amen.*

April 14   **EXODUS 32.25–29**

'Everyone who is on the Lord's side come over here!' (v.26, GNB).

Comment: God was going to keep His promise to the Israelites. He was going to bring them into the promised land. But the people had to make up their minds. Did they really want to follow God—or were they more interested in the golden calf and going their own way? So Moses asks them to make their decision. For those who decided to go their own way rather than look for God's forgiveness there was punishment.

God still wants us to make up our minds. Are we going to follow Him and experience the good things He has for us? Or are we going to go our own way and miss out?

Prayer: *Today, Lord, there will be all sorts of things that lead us away from You. Please help us to follow only You. Amen.*

'Blot me, I pray thee, out of thy book' (v.32, RSV).
Comment: 'If You can't forgive the people,' said Moses, 'kill me.' Whatever gave him that idea? Moses knew that God treated sin very seriously. In fact, the Israelites had special animals called sin offerings. Every time they did something wrong, they put their hands on an innocent animal and thus placing their sins were upon it, too. Then the animal would be killed in place of themselves. As they saw the animal die they would feel sorry for their wrongdoing. But what would be done about such a terrible sin as worshipping false gods? Moses felt that animals were not enough. He, their leader, must offer to die for their sins. Of course God couldn't accept the offer. The only One who could die for men's sins would have to be Someone who had never, ever, done anything wrong Himself.
To talk about together: Who did die for the sins of the whole world? Had He ever done anything wrong?
Prayer: *Thank You, Father, for sending the Lord Jesus to die on the cross for our sins. Amen.*

'Is it not in thy going with us, so that we are distinct . . . ?' (v.16, RSV).
Comment: When Moses went to the tent of meeting to talk to God, all the people went to their doors to watch him. What was it that made Moses different from the others, and which made them so interested in his behaviour? It was his great friendship with God. And what was it about the Israelites which made other nations notice them? It was the fact that God was with them.

What is it that makes Christians different from others in the class, the office, or the neighbourhood? It is the fact that the Lord Jesus is very real to us.
Think: Perhaps you feel people don't even know you are a Christian, or perhaps the Lord Jesus isn't very real to you. Have you a 'tent of meeting'—somewhere where you can go aside to talk to the Lord? Do you use it every day?
Prayer: *Lord Jesus, please help us to know that You are very near, and let other people see by our lives that You are real to us. Amen.*
Sunday extra: Write out the conversation between Moses and God in very simple, modern words and keep it in your Bible to use for your own problems.

Moses said, 'I pray Thee, show me Thy glory' (v.18, RSV).
Comment: 'Do please let me have a look!' You are longing to see
the new baby, or a photograph of someone you have never seen
before, but of whom you have heard enough to make you
thoroughly excited and curious. Of course you want to see for
yourself.

Moses had pleaded for God to stay with them, to lead them on
and show them His way. And God had said that He would.
What a wonderful God He must be! Moses must have remembered vividly the day when he had seen the bush burning, and known
that God was there. Now he longed to see this great God with his
own eyes.

Philip once said to the Lord Jesus, 'Lord, show us the Father,
and we shall be satisfied.' Jesus answered, 'He who has seen me
has seen the Father . . .' The Lord Jesus shows us exactly what
God is like: loving, holy, kind, absolutely fair, angry with sin,
but always wanting to forgive the sinner. We can 'see' Him
today, as we believe in Jesus.
Prayer: *Our Heavenly Father, we praise You because You are
such a wonderful God. Even though we cannot see You with our
eyes, we want to know You in our hearts. Please help our friends
to understand and 'see' You like this. Amen.*

The Lord said to Moses (v.1, RSV).
Comment: We can't get away from it, people are always telling
us to do things at school or at work, in the home, wherever we
are. Sometimes it is the government who tell us to do things like
cutting down on the money we spend or to pay our Income Tax.
Whether we actually do what we are told depends on us. First of
all we think *who* told us to do it and whether they are so important that we feel we should obey. Then we think whether we *agree*
with what we've been told to do. If we don't, we may take no
notice of the instructions we've been given.

Who told Moses to do something (v.1)? What did He tell him
to do (v.2)? What did Moses actually do (v.3)?
Something to discuss: In your own family, can you think of
helpful ways of encouraging one another to do what God wishes
you to do?
Prayer: *Lord God, we don't always find it easy to know exactly
what it is You want us to do, but when we have found that out,
please help us to obey You like Moses did. Amen.*

At the end of forty days they returned from spying out the land (v.25, RSV).
Comment: Moses had told the spies what to look out for. What was the true report of what the spies discovered about: (*1*) the land (vs.26,27)? (*2*) the people (v.28)? (*3*) the cities where the people lived (v.28)?

The spies did not all *feel* the same way about what they had seen. Caleb was hopeful. He said, 'Let's go up and conquer the land. We can do it.' The men who had gone with him felt differently. They were frightened and said, 'We can't fight people as strong as the ones we saw. They were so tall, they made us feel like grasshoppers.'
Something to do: Imagine someone has asked your family to do something and they have said, 'It will not be easy'. What difference do you hope that being a Christian family may make to the way you feel about doing the job?
Prayer: *Heavenly Father, please forgive us for the times we forget that You have promised to be with us, and when we've not had the courage to do what You've wanted because we've been frightened. Amen.*

The idea swept the camp (v.4, Living Bible).
Comment: Research workers, committees of enquiry, Royal Commissions, the Ombudsman and select committees all investigate problems on our behalf and produce 'findings'—just in the same way as the spies produced 'findings' about Canaan. TV, the press, written reports and White Papers spread these 'findings' so that we know about them in the same way as the spies spread news throughout the Israelite camp. All because of the feelings and fears of the spies who did not trust God enough, panic, fear and chaos swept through the lives of ordinary people.
Question: Do you know anyone whose daily work involves finding out about the sort of things that are going to influence people? If so, pray especially for them now.
Prayer: *Lord God, we pray for all research workers and everyone involved in committees of enquiry especially . . . Help them to be accurate and to act with Christian responsibility. Amen.*

'And now, I pray thee, let the power of the Lord be great as thou
hast promised' (v.17, RSV).
Comment: Moses realized that God was angry with the people
because when they had listened to the frightened spies, they had
wanted to take the future into their own hands, and make their
own plans in their own way. When Moses prayed to God he
pleaded for two things.

1. He asked God to continue looking after them so that God's
patient power would be shown to all the pagan nations who did
not serve the same God but were watching God's nation.

2. He asked God, because of His love, to pardon the whole
nation of people for the wrong they had done.
Question: What things do we in our own country need to ask
God to forgive us for?
Prayer: *Heavenly Father, we as a family are part of a nation.
Forgive us when we fail to trust You. Please show Your patient
power again so that others may once more discover that You are
God. Amen.*

But my servant Caleb, because he has a different spirit and has
followed me fully, I will bring into the land into which he went (v.
24, RSV).
Comment: In your family, who is most like Dad? However alike,
you all know that he or she is not the same. Even in the same
family, everyone is different from everyone else. Some of us are
naturally more cheerful, or can play games better, or like being
alone more. But each one of us has a lot to do with what we make
of ourselves.

In Israel there were all sorts of people too. Most of them
grumbled and groused about the way God was treating them,
but Caleb didn't. He took a 'God is with us' view and he was to
receive his reward for this. What was it to be (v.24)?
To discuss: What sort of things can people change about themselves and what can't they change?
Prayer: *Creator God, please help us to handle ourselves in a way
that brings pleasure to You. Amen.*

'. . . because you have turned back from following the Lord, the Lord will not be with you' (v.43, RSV).

Comment: On Friday the Cubs were having a Sausage Sizzle. On Wednesday it poured with rain and Mum told Tim for the tenth time to take his muddy shoes off at the back door but, five minutes later, there was a trail of mud in the kitchen and up the stairs. 'As a punishment,' said Mum, 'you can't go to the Sausage Sizzle.' An hour later Tim sidled up to his mother. 'I'm sorry,' he said. Then, after a pause, 'I can go to the Sausage Sizzle now, can't I?' Tim wasn't really sorry at all, he just wanted to go on Friday. What do the Israelites say in verse 40 that makes them sound like Tim? They knew that God had already told them that they would not get to Canaan themselves. Once more, they were trying to take matters into their own hands.

Question: What is the difference between real sorrow and Tim's kind of sorrow?

Prayer: *Dear Lord, please help us to get into the habit of obeying You rather than into the habit of taking things into our own hands. Amen.*

'Why have you brought the assembly of the Lord into this wilderness, that we should die here . . . ?' (v.4, RSV).

Comment: Mr Grouser is always grumbling about the changes in his office, Mrs Grouser grumbles about rising prices, Tom Grouser grumbles about school lunches and Tina Grouser is always grumbling because she hasn't got the same clothes as her friends. You will have met people like the Grousers.

When we have a problem, there are always at least two ways of coping with it. You can grouse and complain like the Israelites did, or you can see it as an opportunity for God to work wonders and show how powerful He is. Once again, Moses and Aaron took a problem to God. What was it (v.2)?

Question: As a family are you facing any problems that can be shared with God now? If you have a very personal problem, remember to share it with God another time.

Prayer: *Dear God, please help us to see both our personal and family problems as a chance for You to show Your power as You help us to look at them and cope with them. Amen.*

'These are the waters of Meribah' (v.13, RSV). (*Meribah means contention or rebellion.*)

Comment: 'Don't play in the road,' says Mum, 'the traffic is dangerous'. If you rebel, and get run over, you may soon see the result—stitches in your head and a plaster on your arm.

It's not clear what Moses and Aaron did that displeased God although some people think that Moses was boasting when he said *we* in verse 10. What we do know is that after this Moses and Aaron had to live with the knowledge that they, too, would never enter Canaan.

Thought for today: Even if the boy's father and mother forgave him for playing in the road he would still have to live with the cuts and the bruises. It's often like this with sin. If we repent, God has promised to forgive us, but the human result may remain in our life and in the lives of others we've affected.

Prayer: *O God, we find it all too easy to rebel; please help us not to be so easily swayed into wrong ways of thinking and behaving. Amen.*

Aaron shall be gathered to his people (v.24, RSV).

Comment: As we grow up we discover that being sad is not always a bad thing and that it is not always the opposite of being happy about something. Sadness and happiness can belong together and one of the times they can do this is when someone dies. Aaron was dying and that was sad because people were going to miss him; they grieved and cried when he died. For how long (v.29)? But Aaron had a son Eleazar who was going to take his father's place as priest and do his father's work. This is the way in God's world. Grown-ups take care of babies and children until they grow up and are old enough to take their own part in running God's world and then they take over and so the world goes on. This is the good side.

Something to remember: The suffering that sometimes goes with death can be a painful and sad thing. People who suffer need our special love and our prayers.

Prayer: *Heavenly Father, we pray for everyone who is sad because someone they love has died. Please comfort them and help them to see some good things that are happening too. Amen.*

If a serpent bit any man, he would look at the bronze serpent and live (v.9, RSV).

Comment: It's all too easy to grumble today without thinking what it may be like tomorrow. To grumble about working for exams, or about painting the house, without thinking that the qualification will be worth having and the house will be nice to sit in and relax. There's no doubt about it, the Israelites were having a tough time. They complained about the food because there was no variety. They complained that there was not enough to drink. There was disease, illness and death. They got so fed up with the present that they forgot that they were on their way to Canaan where, one day, there would be food and drink and where their children would have the chance of being healthy. Once again, God had to teach them to trust Him.

Questions: What special help did the people need (v.7)? What did they have to do to get it (v.9)?

Prayer: *Dear God, help us to remember that today and its difficulties will pass as we trust You, and that one day we shall be with You in Heaven. Amen.*

And Moab was in great dread of the people, because they were many (v.3, RSV).

Comment: *We* know that the Israelites were having a lot of problems and *we* know that they kept grumbling and that they didn't trust God when they could have done so. None the less to an outsider like Balak, they looked like an enormously strong army and he was very frightened of them.

Because Balak was king of a pagan nation he looked for someone with powerful magic who could put a curse on the Israelites for him. He heard of the diviner Balaam, a man who could see into the future, so he sent him a message. What did he say (v.6)?

Question: Do you think people turn to 'magic' for help nowadays? In what ways? Why do you think this should be avoided?

Prayer: *We have our problems, Lord God, and we don't always obey You as we should, yet we know we are strong when You are with us. Thank You for this. Amen.*

'Lodge here this night, and I will bring back word to you, as the
Lord speaks to me' (v.8, RSV).
Comment: Have you ever noticed that there is a world of difference between the way an ordinary boy or girl, man or woman,
makes up his or her mind about important things and the way a
Christian makes up his or her mind about the same things? For
both sorts of people there may be a lot of thinking to be done, but
for the Christian there is something else as well. Balaam didn't
say 'Yes' and he didn't say 'No' when the elders of Moab and of
Midian came to him; he told them to wait whilst he found out
what God wanted him to do. Then, during the night, God
helped him reason it out.
Something to remember: The next time you have an important
decision to make (1) Ask God what He wants you to do. (2)
Ask God to help you as you think it through so that you reach
the right conclusion.
Prayer: *Father God, please be with us as we think and as we make
decisions today. Amen.*

But God's anger was kindled because he went (v.22, RSV).
Comment: Balaam never told the messengers from Balak *why*
he was not to curse the Israelites. Why was this? (Look back at
verse 12.) This was not something God would change His mind
about. Even so, when the messengers came to offer Balaam more
money, he said he would speak to God once more—almost as if
he thought God might be persuaded to change His mind. Maybe
you have done that before now. It seems as if Balaam really
wanted to go. Perhaps he wanted the money or perhaps he was
frightened about what might happen if he kept on saying 'No'.
When he asked God again he was allowed to go. God chose to
drive home His command in another way. What three things
happened (vs.23,25,27)?
Something to remember: It is because God loves us that He
sometimes chooses to drive His messages home.
Prayer: *Dear God, forgive us for the times when we have asked
You to show us what You wanted us to do and then we've gone and
done what we wanted. Amen.*

'. . . but only the word which I bid you, that shall you speak' (v.35, RSV).

Comment: Life is not always simple and straightforward. People in a muddle look back and say, 'Should I have taken that job in the first place?' or 'Should I have married Andrew?' We can seldom answer these questions with a straight 'Yes' or 'No', so the question to ask is 'What is the best thing to do *now*?'

God sent His angel to interfere with Balaam's journey and it became difficult, uncomfortable and painful, which made him angry. The result was that he was brought face to face with God's wishes again. What did God say (v.35)? Then, later, what did Balaam say to Balak (v.38)?

Let's remember: Every crisis gives us the chance of becoming more the sort of person God wishes us to be—or the opposite.

Prayer: *Lord Jesus, You are able to teach us so many different things in so many different ways. Help us to learn, Lord. Amen.*

'Come, curse Jacob for me, and come, denounce Israel!' (v.7, RSV).

Comment: Today, think back to how the story of Balaam began. What was it that Balak wanted Balaam to do (22.6)? God had told Balaam not to do this because the Israelites were His people and He had blessed them (22.12). Remember how Balaam didn't take this in, and how he hoped that God might be persuaded to change His mind? Balaam had to learn that God was stronger than his own personal wishes. In the situation we've just read about, Balaam was only to do and say what God wanted him to do and say. In the poem which Balaam created under the influence of God, what does *he* say (v.8)?

Something to remember: Have you ever heard someone say 'I think God ought to do so and so . . .'? In the Bible God has shown us the sort of people He loves, He accepts and He turns away, and why He does so.

Prayer: *Heavenly Father, forgive us for the times we think we know better than You do about other people and the way we should behave towards them. Help us to be in touch with Your way. Amen.*

From June 3 to 21 we shall find out more about the instructions which God gave to the Jews—in Deuteronomy. Before that we start reading Luke's Gospel, which we shall read for most of the summer. This will tell us how Jesus came to bring God's new people into existence.

May 3   LUKE 3.1–6

At that time the word of God came to John son of Zechariah in the desert (v.2, GNB).
Comment: Doesn't it seem ages when you are waiting for something special to happen? It may be for a birthday, or even for a shop to open when you've queued for a sale bargain. But at last the time arrives.

For hundreds of years the Jews had been waiting for their own special King to come, and many Old Testament prophets had written about the day when He would at last arrive. Now the right time had come. But just as an earthly king or queen has to have a court official to go ahead to prepare for the royal visit, so Jesus needed a messenger to get things ready for His coming. What a good thing that John was alert and waiting to hear God's orders for the day—and to obey them!
Remember: One day Jesus is coming to earth again. Shall we be ready for Him (John **14.3**)?
Prayer: *Lord, we thank You that You are concerned with the present as well as the past and the future. Help us, like John, to use today to prepare for the coming of Jesus our King. Amen.*

Ascension Day   LUKE 3.15–22

While he was praying, heaven was opened, and the Holy Spirit came down upon him (vs.21,22, GNB).
Comment: How do *you* picture heaven being opened? How it looked isn't really as important as what it means. When the Bible talks about heaven opening it is explaining that God is making contact with men—breaking out of *His* world to get in touch with ours. God urgently wanted to say that Jesus is His Son and the chosen King. He would be with Jesus, through the Holy Spirit, while He lived on earth.

About three years later, heaven opened again for a very different reason. On Ascension Day Jesus left this earth and went back to *God's* world. Very few had recognized Him as King during His life. But God had made Him gloriously alive after death and it was as King of kings that He was welcomed back to heaven.

Prayer: *Lord Jesus, on this happy day we thank You for coming from the joy of heaven to the sadness of earth, to live and die for us. We praise You as the victorious King in God's presence. We look forward to the time when heaven will open again and You will return to earth for those who love You. Amen.*

May 5   **LUKE 4.1–8**

Jesus answered, 'The scripture says, "Man cannot live on bread alone" ' (v.4, GNB).
Comment: Jesus was hungry—hungrier than most of us are ever likely to be—so He did not mean by these words that bread on its own was not good enough to eat, as we might sometimes complain. He used the word 'bread' to stand for food of every kind. He believed that there are some things more important than the good things our bodies enjoy, even though these are part of God's gifts to us. Music and friends, paintings and books are just a few of the important things God has given to us which are likely to last longer than food.

But Jesus' words came from the Old Testament, and the completed verse in Deuteronomy reads, 'Man cannot live on bread alone but lives by every word that comes from the mouth of God' (Deut.8.3, NEB). What God has to say to us in the Bible matters more than anything else in the world.
Question: How can we 'live' on God's words? How does reading *Family Prayers* together help?
Prayer: *Dear Lord Jesus, help us to take Your words in the Bible right into our thoughts and hearts and to obey them today. Amen.*

May 6   **LUKE 4.9–15**

And Jesus answered him, 'It is said . . .' (v.12, RSV).
Comment: 'It must be true because I read it in a book.' 'It can't be, because they said it wasn't on that TV programme.' We may think there are some books or newspapers, programmes or even people whom we can trust completely to tell us the truth, but sooner or later we may find out that they can be wrong or mistaken.

In this story of Jesus' Temptation, we keep finding the phrase, 'It is written' or 'It is said'. Jesus was not talking about just any old book, or any old person's words, but about God's book, the Bible, which He believed to be God's words. As a boy, Jesus would have learned a great deal of the Old Testament by heart at school and now He used it to fight against the evil that the Devil tempted Him to do. We can do the same.

Think Spot: We cannot use the Bible as Jesus did unless we know it. What ways can we think of to begin learning parts of the Bible as a family?

Prayer: *When I am tempted to do wrong today, dear Lord, please bring some words from the Bible to my mind to help me to be strong and do right. For Jesus' sake. Amen.*

May 7   **LUKE 4.16–21**

Then Jesus went to Nazareth, where he had been brought up, and on the Sabbath he went as usual to the synagogue (v.16, GNB).

Comment: Do you sometimes groan at the thought of the same old routine, week in week out, whether at school, work or home? That is one reason why God gave us one day in seven as a special day, when we can be free from the usual chores of daily work. When we use Sunday as just another work day we are missing all the special joy and good to be gained from a day spent differently from the other six.

Jesus kept God's day special, but He had a regular activity for that day too. He went to the synagogue, or church. First His mum would have taken Him, then He chose to keep the habit up. Sunday is God's day before it is ours, and if we love Him we shall want to spend part of it in His house, with others who love Him too.

Sunday Spot: How can we make Sunday special as a family, so that *everyone* has a rest and change?

Prayer: *Dear Father in heaven, You have given us this Sunday. Help us to use it to please You and come to know You better. Amen.*

May 8   **LUKE 4.22–30**

'A prophet is never welcomed in his home town' (v.24, GNB).

Comment: Try to imagine that you had never heard of electricity and then think how excited you would be as someone visiting you from a more advanced country began to tell you about all the wonderful things you could enjoy, once the cables had been laid and the power connected: light, heat, TV, washing machines and so on. Most of us take these things for granted because we have been used to them all our lives.

Jesus' saying about a prophet in his home town meant something like our own proverb: 'Familiarity breeds contempt'.

68

Jesus explained how in olden days great men like Elijah and Elisha were greeted with excitement and trust by foreigners, while their own countrymen took them for granted. Today there are people in other lands who are learning about Jesus for the first time with terrific thrill and putting their full trust in Him. **Question:** Are we so used to the stories of Jesus in our family that we no longer see Him as the One who can meet our needs? **Prayer:** *Lord Jesus, help us to see You with fresh eyes today and to welcome You into our hearts and into our family. Amen.*

May 9   **LUKE 4.31-37**

They were astonished at his teaching, for his word was with authority (v.32, RSV).
Comment: 'If it happens again, you'll go straight to bed,' says Dad or Mum. 'If you don't stop this row you'll stay in all break,' says the history teacher. Perhaps you think grown-ups' threats are unfair, when you are at the receiving end of them. But you still obey, if you know that the person who has made the threat has the power and right to carry it out. That's what authority means—the right to give orders *and* the power to see that they are obeyed.

Jesus had absolute authority over people because as well as being a man He is also God, who created and rules over everything. But Jesus did not throw His weight about, like some new prefects do, keeping people under His control. He used His power to fight evil and teach the truth about God.
Think: What place does authority have in our family? Parents have been given authority to use for the family good and should be obeyed without fuss. But parents must use that authority wisely. See Ephesians 6.1-4.
Prayer: *Dear Lord Jesus, help all of us in our family to put ourselves under Your authority and to find happiness in obeying You. Amen.*

May 10   **LUKE 4.38-44**

Jesus left the synagogue and went to Simon's house (v.38, GNB).
Comment: When someone is ill—really ill—the whole family routine is upset. Very often it's specially worrying for the mother of the family who may be doing most of the nursing, as well as going to work and trying to do the usual jobs. It certainly isn't a time for inviting visitors to dinner.

I wonder whether Peter's wife felt it was just too much when

69

her husband brought Jesus back to lunch after synagogue service. It wasn't even as if there was a best room to put Him in. Their house would have had only one room for eating and sleeping, for the family and the animals, as well as for poor sick Gran. Perhaps Peter's wife realized that Jesus was no ordinary guest, for they told Him the whole story and let Him take charge. Jesus soon brought back happiness and order to the whole household.

Question: Do we together invite Jesus to come in on all our family problems and difficulties, however large or small?

Prayer: *Lord Jesus, come and live in our home, not as a visitor but as the One who is in charge of all that goes on. Amen.*

May 11   LUKE 5.1–11

Getting into one of the boats, which was Simon's, he asked him to put out a little from the land (v.3, RSV).

Comment: Perhaps it's easier to think of Jesus being in our home than to realize that He wants to be with us where we work too. As well as being in Peter's house, Jesus was down on the beach among the fishing boats. We may not be as surprised as the fishermen were that Jesus could help them with their job, and that He knew more about it than they did; but it *is* surprising to think that Jesus needed *their* help too.

The crowds had jostled so close to Him that Jesus could not make His voice heard by all. So He borrowed Peter's boat, and Peter's strength to push the boat, and talked to the crowds from off the shore. Jesus can use our skills and possessions if we let Him, as well as helping us with our work, in school, office, factory, hospital or wherever it may be.

Question: Does Jesus want to use our typewriter, cooker or car to bring His love to others today?

Prayer: *Lord Jesus, come into the world of our everyday work today. Use all we have, and help us to do our work well because we do it for You. Amen.*

May 12   LUKE 5.12–16

When he saw Jesus, he threw himself down and begged him, 'Sir, if you want to, you can make me clean!' (v.12, GNB).

Comment: If I asked you the opposite of 'ill' you would probably say 'well', and of 'dirty' you would answer 'clean'. What an odd thing it seems for someone ill to ask to be made 'clean' rather than 'well'! But to Jews, brought up on the rules of the Old

Testament, leprosy was not just an illness. It was one of the things which made a person unfit to come to God—just as filthy rags would make someone unfit for a king's presence. So when Jesus healed the leper, He not only made him well in body but fit to go to God's house again.

We sometimes talk about the wrong things we do or say or think as making us 'dirty' in God's sight—unfit to come near Him. Jesus is able to make us clean from all the wrong things on our consciences so that we can be free from stain and guilty feelings.

Thought: It's easy for me to ask Jesus for forgiveness, but it cost Jesus His life to take away my sin.

Prayer: *Lord, make us clean from all that has spoiled and stained us in thought, word and action today. Amen.*

May 13   **LUKE 5.17–26**

When Jesus saw how much faith they had, he said to the man, 'Your sins are forgiven, my friend' (v.20, GNB).

Comment: What a lot of trouble those men had taken to bring their friend to Jesus! They had pushed their way through the crowd with a heavy stretcher, scrambled to the flat roof with their load and even managed to lower the invalid into the room where Jesus was. And all so that Jesus would heal his illness. How must they have felt when Jesus talked about forgiving sins? *That* wasn't what they had in mind at all.

But Jesus always puts first things first. *He* knew, though the friends did not, that the paralysed man had a bigger problem than his useless body. He needed healing and forgiveness for wrong things he had done. So Jesus saw to that first, then gave him back the use of his body too.

Saturday Spot: What does Jesus see as the greatest need in *our* family? A new carpet? A summer holiday? Or less bickering and more kindness and help to one another?

Prayer: *Lord Jesus, You can meet our deepest needs as a family. Please put right what You see needs changing and give us such benefits of life as may be good for us. Amen.*

Whit Sunday   **ACTS 2.1–11**

Then they saw what looked like tongues of fire which spread out and touched each person there (v.3, GNB).

Comment: 'I can't be in two places at once,' Mum says. She wants to be at Denise's Swimming Gala *and* at Janet's PTA 'Bring

71

and Buy', but they are both on the same evening! Have you ever thought that Jesus Himself had this problem when He was on earth? We read how the crowds in one village wanted Him to stay, but He said He must go to others who had not had a chance to meet Him. He couldn't do both.

Whit Sunday tells us that now Jesus can be with *everyone* at the same time. When He went back to God, Jesus promised to send His Spirit to be with His disciples. The tongues of fire that the disciples saw were a sign that Jesus had kept His word. *Each* person felt the presence of Jesus coming to them. And the best of it was that the Holy Spirit had come to stay.

Thought: Today, through His Holy Spirit, Jesus lives within everyone who loves Him, wherever they may be.

Prayer: *Thank You, Lord Jesus, for sending Your Spirit into our hearts. May we listen to His quiet voice and know His help today. Amen.*

May 15   **LUKE 5.27–32**

Then Levi had a big feast in his house for Jesus, and among the guests was a large number of tax collectors and other people (v.29, GNB).

Comment: I wonder if yours is the kind of home where people are always dropping in for tea or supper, or to play in the garden, with biscuits and orange juice in the kitchen afterwards. You may not give many special parties or dinners, like Levi did, but there often seem to be extra people at the meal table.

Levi threw his party specially for Jesus and asked all his old work-mates and friends so that they could meet Jesus too. In some Christian homes today you see a framed verse which says, 'Jesus is the unseen Guest at every meal'. Whether we put up such a notice or not, if we *behave* as if Jesus is present, all our visitors from work, school or next door, will notice.

Question: What difference will the presence of Jesus make to our meal times and our parties?

Prayer: *Lord Jesus, You never go where You are not wanted. We ask You to come to our home and be present at every family meal and every special occasion. May our friends meet You through coming to our home. Amen.*

'New wine must be poured into fresh wineskins!' (v.38, GNB).
Comment: In the days before glass bottles, people used animal
skins to hold wine or water. New-made wine always goes on
expanding, but a new animal skin was elastic enough to swell
with the wine. If an old, already stretched, skin was used to
hold new wine, it had no stretch left and burst as soon as the
new wine expanded. I expect Jesus and His hearers had seen the
kind of mess *that* could cause in a nice clean kitchen!

Jesus' teaching about God was brand new, like new wine.
It was too bubbling and exciting to be made to fit into the cold,
hard limits of the Pharisees' religion. But, sadly, most of the
religious people preferred the old ways and had no patience with
the overflowing happiness and the unconventional ways of Jesus
and His followers.

Question: Does the set way of life in our family cramp and limit
the freedom and happiness that Jesus' teaching of love should
bring?

Prayer: *Lord Jesus, You came to give us life abundant, full and
free from fear. Give us the courage to live that way to Your glory
and the blessing of others. Amen.*

Some Pharisees asked, 'Why are you doing what our Law says you
cannot do on the Sabbath?' (v.2, GNB).
Comment: Robert and Mark met Mrs Smith struggling up the
hill with her shopping as they were walking home from school.
Mark stopped to carry her bags to her front gate and got home
late. Robert said *he'd* done what Mum told them by going *straight*
home. Mum said she was pleased with Mark because he had
helped poor Mrs Smith, which was more important than keeping
her rule just for once.

When Jesus saw the Pharisees pretending they were pleasing
God by keeping His rules, when they didn't care tuppence for
one of God's children, it made Him angry and sad. He knew that
God cared far more that the crippled man should be helped than
that people should stick to the hundred and one rules that had
been added to God's Sabbath law.

Question: Do our family rules—about meal times, TV, or leisure
—ever hinder us from showing love and giving help to people
who need it?

Prayer: *Dear Father, help us to put our love for You, and our*

*thoughtfulness and care for others who are in need, before our own
pet rules or family routine. Open our eyes to see when others need
our help. Amen.*

May 18   **LUKE 6.12–19**

**When day came, he called his disciples to him and chose twelve
of them** (v.13, GNB).
Comment: David was pleased because he had been chosen to play
football in the school team. Rosemary, his little sister, was just
as excited at being asked to play the recorder at the music
festival. Dad hoped he'd be selected to represent his firm on a
trade mission and Mum was glad to be voted on to the PTA
committee. Everyone likes to be *chosen*; it means that someone
thinks we are worthy of notice and good for the job in hand.
How pleased the twelve apostles must have been to be chosen
by Jesus Himself to be His special friends and messengers!

Perhaps we think of following Jesus as something *we* choose
to do, but the Bible often reminds us that it is God who chooses
us. He loves us and wants us enough to ask us to be in *His* team
for always.
Remember: We need not be afraid that Jesus has not chosen us.
Those who are willing and ready to serve Him can be sure that
they have been chosen already.
Prayer: *Thank You, Lord Jesus, for choosing us to be Your
followers. Help us gladly to say 'Yes' to You and to be faithful and
obedient to You always. Amen.*

May 19   **LUKE 7.1–10**
**'I order this one, "Go!" and he goes; I order that one, "Come!"
and he comes; and I order my slave, "Do this!" and he does it'**
(v.8, GNB).
Comment: How many in your family enjoy telling the rest what
to do? Quite a few people seem to get bossy if they are given half
a chance, and they can get a bit above themselves if they are put
in charge.

The Roman officer in today's story may seem like that at first.
He was certainly used to giving orders and said that he was used
to having them obeyed at once. But instead of becoming stuck-
up or self-important, he had learned through his job how to *take*
orders from those higher up. He didn't expect Jesus to be impressed with him or to fit in with his demands. He recognized
Jesus as Someone far greater than he was, and believed that even
illness and death must be obedient to *Him*.

Question: Are we learning, in family, school and work, both to give and to obey orders in the right spirit?
Prayer: *Lord Jesus, Your power and authority are as great today as when You met the Roman officer. Help us to believe, as he did, that You can control the evil that we will face today. Amen.*

May 20   LUKE 7.11–17

When the Lord saw her, his heart was filled with pity for her, and he said to her, 'Don't cry' (v.13, GNB).
Comment: When Mr Smith, across the road, died, no one knew what to say to Mrs Smith. Mrs Brown crossed the road quickly so that she would not have to speak to her, and Mrs Jones just chatted brightly about the weather when she met her in the super-market. Everyone was sorry but too shy or too busy to do any-thing for Mrs Smith. The Roberts' family felt shy too, but asked God to show them how to help. They knew Mrs Smith would be alone on Sundays now, so they asked her to dinner and tea. Mrs Smith was glad to talk everything over with Mrs Roberts while Mr Roberts washed up, and then she enjoyed playing with Tim's trains and helping with Joanna's jigsaw. So all the family shared Mrs Smith's sadness, as Jesus did with the widow at Nain.
Remember: Jesus' miracle reminds us that Jesus has overcome death. Those who love Him will one day have a wonderful new body and will live with Him for ever after death.
Prayer: *Lord, please show us how to comfort those who are sad today because one they love has died. Give us Your pity and understanding. Amen.*

May 21   LUKE 7.18–23

'How happy are those who have no doubts about me!' (v.23, GNB).
Comment: Many people these days have doubts about Jesus Christ. They believe that He once lived, but they doubt that He was God's Son or that He rose from the dead. Teachers and friends may try to persuade us that it is silly or out of date to believe in Jesus as the writers of the New Testament did.

Poor John the Baptist, alone in Herod's dark and filthy dungeon, had plenty of cause for growing downhearted. That led him to doubt whether Jesus was really the King that John had proclaimed. Jesus did not tell John off, but sent a message describing all the ways in which He was healing and helping people. Jesus' power over illness and evil proved He was indeed the King. Jesus still lives within those who love Him and when we are tempted to doubt, we can look at the changed lives of Christians and read some of the books that tell true life stories.

Thought: Will other people be ready to believe in Jesus because of what they see Him doing in *our* family?

Prayer: *Lord Jesus, when we are tempted to doubt You, help us to know that You are near, and to enjoy Your peace and strength. Amen.*

May 22   **LUKE 7.36–50**

'If this man really were a prophet, he would know who this woman is who is touching him; he would know what kind of sinful life she lives!' (v.39, GNB).

Comment: *'She's* stupid!'; *'He's* hopeless at sport!'; 'You should see the way she keeps her house!'; *'They're* coloured!'; *'He* hasn't much of a job!' Doesn't it sound horrid when other people are snobbish or prejudiced like that? Yet we are all sometimes tempted to look down on other people, even though it may not be for any of the reasons mentioned above, and though we may keep our thoughts to ourselves. People who go to church, like this Pharisee, have sometimes despised those who are not religious or who lead bad, immoral lives.

Simon the Pharisee thought himself a cut above the woman who had cared for Jesus' needs, and he expected Jesus to feel the same way. But Jesus saw into both their hearts and knew the love and penitence in the woman's heart and the coldness and pride in Simon's.

Remember: God hates sin, but He loves us all—and we are *all* sinners.

Prayer: *Lord, save me from looking down on any fellow human beings. Give me a sense of my own sinfulness and make me warm and caring towards others, because I love You. Amen.*

May 23   **LUKE 8.1–8**

'Let the man who has ears to hear use them!' (v.8, J.B. Phillips).
Comment: I turned on the radio specially to hear the weather forecast but when the news began I realized that I had not heard a word. There wasn't anything wrong with my ears, but I hadn't been using them. Plenty of girls and boys do the same in class, even though they manage to look quite intent on what is being said.

Jesus knew that the crowds would find it easy to listen to His parables, but it would be a case of 'in one ear and out the other'. They did not care about the meaning behind the stories, nor were they willing to take to heart the lessons they taught. When we *really* listen, we let what we hear make a difference to the way we behave. If I had listened to the forecast I would have worn my raincoat and not got wet!

Thought: God has something to say to me today from His Word. Am I listening?

Prayer: *Lord, help us never to close our minds to what Your Word says because we are lazy or because we are not willing to obey. Give us listening ears and obedient hearts. Amen.*

May 24   LUKE 8.9–15

'The worries and riches and pleasures of this life crowd in' (v.14, GNB).

Comment: Born worriers always find something to worry about, but mums and dads have a good excuse for worrying because they have so many responsibilities. We may all have worries though we certainly haven't all got riches; but what money we *have* got may take up a lot of our thoughts, and the money we'd *like* to have, or plan to earn, can take up still more. And pleasures?—Well, after all, it's only natural to want to enjoy ourselves when we're young, and when we're older we need to relax.

Jesus is not saying that either money or pleasure is wrong, though worry for a Christian often is. He is telling us that if these are the things that crowd our minds, there will be no room left for God. After all, a life taken up with *my* concerns and *my* good times is a life with myself, not Jesus Christ, at the centre.

Think Spot: Notice what Jesus says we must do with God's Word if we are to show the results in our lives (see v.15).

Prayer: *Heavenly Father, when we are tempted to worry today, help us to remember that You know and care about us and are great enough to provide for our needs. Amen.*

May 25   LUKE 8.16–25

Jesus ... gave an order to the wind and the stormy water; they died down and there was a great calm (v.24, GNB).

Comment: 'I don't know what's wrong with our family,' Mum said, 'you never see that family over the road quarrelling. They always seem so happy together.'

'*Their* mum and dad don't shout at them all the time,' Mike muttered.

Mum sighed. They really did seem to be having a lot of rows.

77

Perhaps there *are* some families where all is sweetness and light, but most families quarrel at times though probably not when *we* see them. So what can be done? No one likes a home which is always full of storms, even though we may not expect smooth sailing all the time. If we think of our family unit as being in the same boat together, then we can do as the disciples and see that we have Jesus on board. When things are really bad and we all feel mad at one another *He* can bring calmness. Next time there is a row, why not ask Jesus to take away our anger and selfishness and bring His peace?

Resolution: To pray together, whatever the trouble.

Prayer: *Lord Jesus Christ, take away our selfishness and pride and give peace in our family today. Amen.*

May 26   **LUKE 8.26–33**

As Jesus stepped ashore, he was met by a man from the town who had demons in him (v.27, GNB).

Comment: Have you ever taken part in a tug-of-war, or watched one taking place at school sports? Sometimes it's a while before you can tell which side is going to win. Then, gradually, the stronger side gains ground and finally pulls the other side right over.

Some people feel that the world is a bit like a tug-of-war between good and evil, where it often looks as if bad is winning. But the coming of Jesus tells us that it is no such thing. Jesus, God's Son, is stronger than any force of evil and He has won the battle already. The poor man in this story was under the power of very great evil, but Jesus was stronger and could save him from it.

Explanation: Perhaps you feel sorry for the pigs. Jesus wanted the man he had healed to know *for sure* that the demons had left him for good. Seeing the pigs running madly would convince him that he was cured. Jesus believed that people were more important than pigs.

Prayer: *Thank You, Lord Jesus, for overcoming all the powers of evil. Please give me Your help to fight wrong today. Amen.*

May 27   **LUKE 8.34–39**

'Go back home and tell what God has done for you' (v.39, GNB).

Comment: I wonder what *your* home is like? Perhaps you live in a busy city in a high rise flat. You may be on a large housing estate in a small town, where neighbours are always dropping in.

Or you may have a cottage in a village, with a mile to walk to the bus. God has put Christians in all kinds of places because that way all kinds of people can come to hear about Jesus through their neighbours. Our home is the right place for us to begin to tell others about Him.

The way we set about it will depend on the kind of home and family we have. Some may hold Bible Study groups or Youth Fellowships in their sitting rooms; others have lonely folk in for a cup of tea. Many people are discovering again that the home is the best centre for spreading the good news, as it was in the days of the early church.

Think Spot: Discuss some new way in which you could use your home to tell others what God has done for you.

Prayer: *Lord, we offer You our home. Please take it and show us how to use it to tell others about You. Amen.*

May 28   **LUKE 8.40–48**

He threw himself down at Jesus' feet and begged him to go to his home (v.41, GNB).

Comment: If you are waiting at an airport for the arrival of your favourite pop group, or standing along the route where a member of the royal family will drive by, you are content to see and be near the person you admire. You don't *really* expect them— except in wild day-dreams—to accept an invitation to visit your home. Jesus was surrounded by thronging, welcoming crowds; far too busy, we would think, to spend time at the home of any one person.

Do you ever feel that God must be far too great and busy to bother with what is happening in your home? The actions of Jesus show us that this is not true. He went with Jairus straight away. He always had time for any one who needed His help. He's the same today.

Remember: Whatever the problem or need in our home, we can ask Jesus to come and deal with it and He will.

Prayer: *Lord, we often don't know what is going on in other people's homes. We ask You to help those with special needs and sadness in their home today and to give them the comfort of Your presence. For Jesus' sake. Amen.*

Jesus ... said to Jairus, 'Don't be afraid; only believe' (v.50, GNB).

Comment: I wonder what *you* are afraid of? Often we don't let on to anyone about our deepest fears, but all of us have them. We may be afraid of some person, or some activity, at school. When we are older we may be afraid of losing our job; of not being able to pay the bills; of failing an exam.; of growing old or ill. Sometimes, like Jairus, our fears are not for ourselves but for someone we love very much.

Jesus will always understand our fears and the best thing we can do is to share them with Him. He will not always take away the thing we fear straight away, as we would like, but He has promised to give us His peace and to be with us always. We know too that He can bring something good from all that happens to us. He loves us too much to allow anything to befall but what is best for us in the long run.

Note: Jesus gave Jairus something else to do instead of being afraid (see v.50). We can do the same today.

Prayer: *Lord Jesus, help us to believe and put our full trust in You today, whatever our fears may be. Amen.*

O taste and see that the Lord is good! Happy is the man who takes refuge in him! (v.8, RSV).

Comment: Are you reading these notes at a meal-time—perhaps breakfast or supper? It may be that Mum has cooked something new today, and the fussy members of your family have been suspicious and didn't want to eat it. Then someone said, 'This is great, you ought to try it!' And everyone ended up by thoroughly enjoying it and asking Mum to make it again. We like to pass on good news from one to another. We see a thing, look at it carefully, test it out and then shout about it. Our appreciation can help someone else to appreciate it too. The gospel is often spread in this way. Those who have experienced the wonder and joy of belonging to Jesus and having their sins forgiven can't help talking about it. That's how I heard about Jesus and became a Christian myself.

To think about: The more we share the good news of Jesus Christ with others, the more it multiplies.

Prayer: *Lord Jesus, forgive us for all the wasted years in which we have hesitated to taste and see how good You really are. Amen.*

Evil shall slay the wicked; and those who hate the righteous will be condemned (v.21, RSV).

Comment: At one time the saying, 'Crime doesn't pay' was agreed with by almost everybody. Today, many people live as though it was no longer true. Fines can be paid so easily and prison sentences are so short for the most terrible offences that those who do wrong really do seem to get away with it. Have you ever played with a boomerang? It was fun to throw it up and see it come back within reach again, wasn't it? There is a kind of boomerang which is deadly serious and its name is 'evil'. It may take quite a long time but eventually it always comes back upon the wicked. If that 'evil' has been aimed at one of God's servants, the psalmist tells us that the Lord will come to his rescue, so that he is not really harmed. But the psalmist also says that God turns His face against evildoers and they are destroyed.

Question: Were we intending to act or speak against someone today? Remember the boomerang!

Prayer: *We thank You, Lord, that while evil has a way of making wicked people miserable and invites Your anger, You deliver from harm those who put their trust in You. Amen.*

May God be gracious to us and bless us and make his face to shine upon us, that thy way may be known upon earth, thy saving power among all nations (vs.1, 2, RSV).

Comment: It is not part of God's plan that any Christian should be like a terminus or a dead end. He wants us to be more like a junction so that He can send His message out in all directions. A goods yard on the railway is not a place for storing lots of boxes and parcels, but a place for sorting them and sending them on. God doesn't bless us with His gift of salvation and then put us in our cosy little home church fellowship or Sunday school so that we can keep it all to ourselves. He wants us to share the good news with those people outside who don't know or understand what Christianity is all about—and that includes all nations too. We have to be an international junction for God.

Question: Is our home a terminus? If so, we'd better get back down the line: there's work to be done.

Prayer: *Forgive us, Lord, for wasting time instead of getting on with the job. Help us to make Your way known upon earth. Amen.*

Thy throne is established from of old; thou art from everlasting (v.2, RSV).

Comment: 'Established since 1798' it said over the shop, which suggested that this very old firm could be trusted. 'Please may I speak to the manager?' asked a customer after having been passed from one assistant to another without satisfaction. The assistants may have been a bit scatter-brained but the manager was on top of the job. Christianity must appear rather like that to non-Christians. We servants of God do our best but we don't always find answers when people come to us with their problems, and we don't always give the same answers as one another. We are often afraid to admit that we don't know what advice to give, but we can put our enquiring friends in touch with God who manages the universe. He has been established since before everything began, and by our praying and searching the Bible, God will make His answers known.

Thought: 'For every one who asks receives, and he who seeks finds, and to him who knocks it will be opened' (Matthew 7.8).

Prayer: *Eternal Father, make us into useful servants and help us to put people in touch with You. For Jesus' sake. Amen.*

'Never favour a man because he is rich; be fair to great and small alike. Don't fear their displeasure, for you are judging in the place of God' (v.17, Living Bible).

Comment: 'It's not fair! If John's going on holiday with the school, why can't I?'

'Jill won't let me ride on the bike and we're supposed to share it.'

All families have their problems and quarrels. Sometimes we need other people to sort them out and decide who is right and who is wrong.

Even God's special people, about to enter the land God had promised them, had their quarrels. Moses chose men to judge the rights and wrongs of arguments. In verse 17 he tells them how they should judge.

It's very important when we have to make similar decisions that we should be fair to everyone. We should remember that God doesn't have favourites just because they are bigger or shout louder. It's no good just judging by appearances—we need to find out the facts.

Prayer: *Father God, please help us to make wise and fair decisions just as Moses' helpers did. Amen.*

'The Lord God has given us this land. Go and possess it as he told us to. Don't be afraid. Don't even doubt!' (v.21, Living Bible).

Comment: 'Come on; jump. I'll catch you,' shouts Dad. But Jo stands shivering on the edge of the swimming pool. She longs to jump in and share the fun, but she's scared of the water. So she turns back into the changing-room, and misses all the fun.

So often we miss the best things in life because we worry about what might happen instead of trusting God. If God tells us to do something, then we can safely 'jump in' and do it. God is far more reliable than any human father, and He wants the very best for us.

Sunday Search: Look up the story of two men who dared to obey God (Acts 4.16–20).

Prayer: *Lord God, please help us not to doubt Your great love for us. May we be willing to go along with Your plans for our lives day by day. Amen.*

They murmured and complained in their tents and said, 'The Lord must hate us . . .' They refused to believe the Lord our God who had led them all the way (vs.27, 32, Living Bible).

Comment: Sally rushes upstairs, slams her door, and sobs, 'I don't want to go to a new school.' Dad comes in and throws down his brief-case. 'I wish I'd never got that promotion. More trouble than it's worth.' 'I wish we weren't moving house,' sighs Mum. 'I dread meeting new neighbours.'

God was leading this family to something new and exciting and promising. But all they could do was complain—just like the people of Israel on the border of the promised land.

Something to do: Talk about the ways God has led you recently and about any decision you may soon need to make.

Prayer: *Forgive us, Father, for the times when we complain about what You are doing for us. Please guide us in everything and help us to follow You gladly. Amen.*

'I will give the land to the children . . . But as for you of the older generation, turn around now and go back across the desert toward the Red Sea' (vs.39, 40, Living Bible).

Comment: Do you ever change your mind when it is too late?

You decide you will help with the washing up just as the last plate has been dried.

You decide you will apologize to the person to whom you were rude, only to find they've left before you got round to it.

The older generation of the people of Israel had moaned and groaned about the job God was giving them to do. They kept saying how difficult it was, instead of getting on with it. It wasn't until God took the opportunity away and told them their children would be the ones to enter the promised land that they changed their minds. But then it was too late.

Prayer: *Lord God, when we are sure of what You want us to do, please help us to do it at once and not leave it until it is too late. Amen.*

June 7   DEUTERONOMY 6.1–9

'Think constantly about these commandments I am giving you today. You must teach them to your children and talk about them when you are at home or out for a walk; at bedtime and the first thing in the morning' (vs.6,7, Living Bible).

Comment: Family prayers is not a modern invention. Over four thousand years ago, families were getting together, night and morning, to think about God's Word. And they were talking about it. Important lessons can be learnt if we take time to answer each other's questions about God whenever they crop up.

Think: Is it enough to leave our learning from God's Word to 'chance' conversations? Shouldn't we also organize our time to include regular Bible study?

Prayer: *Thank You, Lord, for every opportunity we have of learning more about You. Please help us to use them wisely. Amen.*

June 8   DEUTERONOMY 6.10–19

Beware lest you forget the Lord who brought you out of the land of Egypt, the land of slavery (v.12, Living Bible).

Comment: When we've got exams, or a big match; when somebody is very ill, or there's been an accident . . . then we pray. But when things are going well . . . we passed the exam, won the match and Dad has recovered from his operation . . . do we remember to pray then?

Prayer shouldn't be just a list of requests. God wants us to thank Him for the good things He's given us, too, and He wants us to remember to talk to Him in bad and good times.

Prayer: *Heavenly Father, we are glad that You are always ready to hear our prayers.*
Now talk to God about the things your family will be doing today.

June 9   **DEUTERONOMY 6.20–25**

'We saw it all with our own eyes. He brought us out of Egypt so that He could give us this land' (vs.22, 23, Living Bible).
Comment: For a Jewish boy history was a most important subject. It was like a secret code which gave important information about the present and the future. Most important of all, history was the story of what God had done for His people. Looking back to the wonderful way God had freed them from slavery in Egypt and brought them to the promised land, helped the people to remember what a great God they served.

As we think about God, and all that He has done for us in the past, that should make us all the more ready to obey Him now.
Prayer: *Lord God, thank You that nothing is too difficult for You. Help us to remember that as we try to obey You today. Amen.*

June 10   **DEUTERONOMY 8.1–10**

'When you have eaten your fill, bless the Lord your God for the good land he has given you' (v.10, Living Bible).
Comment: How often do you leave the table still feeling hungry? Most of us are more likely to have had too much to eat than too little. Do you ever leave the table grumbling because it was not your favourite meal? Many people would be very grateful to have had anything to eat at all.

We should always be thankful to God for the way He gives us so much good food. We need to find practical ways, too, in which we can help to provide food for those in countries where agriculture is not so developed as in our country.
Something to do: Find out about ways in which you can help in the work of TEAR Fund or other organizations which are trying to help people who do not have enough to eat.
Prayer: *We are sorry, heavenly Father, for the times when we are ungrateful. Please help us to remember how good You are to us. Amen.*

'Always remember that it is the Lord your God who gives you power to become rich . . .' (v.18, Living Bible).

Comment: 'Top of the class again! That was clever of me, wasn't it?' 'Another rise—I'm doing pretty well for myself these days.' Does anyone in your family ever say things like that? When we have done well we always like to feel a little bit proud. We begin to think that it is all as a result of what we have done.

God knew that when the Israelites came into the promised land they would get much richer. So He warned them to remember that this was only because of all the advantages *He* had given them. When we do well it is because of the abilities and opportunities that God has given us. He wants us to work hard and do the best we can with them—but He doesn't want us to get the idea that we have done it all by ourselves.

Prayer: *Dear Lord, thank You for the abilities and opportunities that You give us. Please help us to use them properly and never to be proud. Amen.*

'At the end of every seventh year there is to be a cancelling of all debts!' (v.1, Living Bible).

Comment: If you are buying the house you live in maybe you had to borrow some money from a Building Society or Insurance Company. If so it will take you a long time to pay it back. Wouldn't it be nice if after seven years there was nothing more to pay? That is what would have happened if you had lived in Israel.

Our society is very different and it wouldn't always be right to try to use the Jewish regulations today. But it is important to realize why God gave His people this rule. He didn't want some to become very rich while others became very poor—and that is still true. He wants people to care for one another and share what He has given them.

Think: How can you as a family do something to show God's care for the poor?

Prayer: *Help us, dear Lord, never to be greedy or selfish but always to be generous and fair with everyone. Amen.*

'You must lend him what he needs, and don't moan about it
either!' (v.10, Living Bible).
Comment: 'All right, then, if you must. But I get a bit sick of
people borrowing my things.'
   'We'll have to cut down our donation this year if we're going
to buy a new TV set.'
   Even if we do consider the needs of others, we are often less
than generous and enthusiastic in our giving.
   The New Testament reminds us that, 'the Lord loves a cheerful
giver' (2 Corinthians 9.7). He promised to bless the people of
Israel if they were generous and ungrudging towards poorer
people, and He will certainly bless us, too, if we act in the same
way.
Prayer: *Father God, You know that sometimes we are not very
willing to share our money and possessions. Help us to remember
that everything we have comes from You and help us to share what
we have cheerfully with others. Amen.*

Don't send your slave away empty-handed. Give him a large fare-
well present . . . When you free a slave you must not feel bad
(vs.13, 14, 18, Living Bible).
Comment: It may surprise you to find that the people of God
kept slaves. In those days no one would have questioned this.
Many slaves were treated very cruelly. But God said that His
people were to be kind and generous to their slaves. They should
be well looked after and when they were freed they were to be
given a present that would help them to set up on their own.
   God still expects employers to treat those who work for them
fairly. They should pay good wages and make sure that there are
reasonable working conditions.
Think: Have you read about (or seen on TV) any groups of
people who are not being fairly treated? Is there anything you
can do about this?
Prayer: *We pray, Lord, for all those who are being unfairly
treated. Please make them strong and patient and help Your people
to stand out against unfairness wherever they find it. Amen.*

'. . . be sure you select as king the man the Lord your God shall choose' (v.15, Living Bible).

Comment: 'Sandra is very popular—she'd make a good Bible Class leader.' 'Mrs. Stewart has a big house and plenty of money. We ought to have her on the church council.' When we have to choose someone for an important job how do we make the decision?

God knew that when His people had settled down in the promised land they would want a king. Perhaps they should choose the strongest, or the richest, or the cleverest.

'No,' says God, 'you must have the one I choose.' And that is how we, too, should select people, especially for jobs in the church.

Think: What questions should we ask when we are trying to see if someone is the right person to take on a job in the church?

Prayer: *Thank You, Lord, for having people to do all the jobs that need to be done. Help us to choose the right people and not just follow our own ideas. Amen.*

This regular reading of God's laws will prevent him from feeling that he is better than his fellow-citizens (v.20, Living Bible).

Comment: It's very easy for leaders to feel that they are better than other people, isn't it? Perhaps you think you know people like that—but then perhaps you feel that *you* are better than someone else.

It would do us all good to read God's laws more often, like the king of Israel had to. Then we would realize just how often we failed. We wouldn't be able to think we were better than other people then. None of us has kept God's law as He wants us to.

Prayer: *Help us, Lord, never to think of ourselves as better than other people. Please be with all our leaders and help them, too. Amen.*

'They don't need to own property, for the Lord is their property!' (v.2, Living Bible).

Comment: Do you know any missionaries? Are they rich people with big houses and new cars? Probably not—and probably your own minister or vicar doesn't own his house either.

The priests and Levites had the special job of looking after the Temple and organizing the worship. They didn't have any land of their own but God promised to look after them. Most missionaries today will tell you the same. And they often have wonderful stories to tell of the way God has met their needs.

Something to do: The Levites were supported from the offerings brought by God's people. So are modern missionaries. Does your family support any missionaries? If so, find out all you can about them and their needs. If not, why not think about it today?

Prayer: *Be with all missionaries today, dear Lord, especially those who have special needs. Remind them of Your power to help them. Amen.*

June 18   DEUTERONOMY 19.1–10

'You must set apart three Cities of Refuge, so that anyone who accidentally kills someone may flee to safety . . . Anyone seeking to avenge the death will not be able to' (vs.3, 6, Living Bible).

Comment: 'I'll get my brother on to you! He's bigger than you are!' Have you ever heard something like that said at school? If one member of a family gets 'beaten up' the others often want to get their revenge. And they don't always stop to think about the rights and wrongs of the matter.

This is what was happening in today's reading. When someone was killed his family would set out looking for revenge. If they caught the killer they might not wait for a fair trial—even though the death might have been a complete accident. So God told the Israelites to set aside these cities, so that everyone could be sure of a fair trial.

To think about: In most countries today there is a system which sees that justice is done. How does it operate in your country?

Prayer: *Thank You, Father, for all those who run our legal system—police, lawyers, judges and others. Please help them to be completely fair. Amen.*

June 19   DEUTERONOMY 19.11–14

'When you arrive in the land the Lord your God is giving you remember that you must never steal a man's land by moving the boundary marker' (v.14, Living Bible).

Comment: The previous owner of our house put up a new fence. But she didn't put it in place of the old one; she moved it six inches. By doing this she stole a strip of extra flower bed.

This is similar to what God is warning the Israelites against here. They didn't always use fences. Sometimes the boundary of the land would be marked with a heap of stones. It would be very easy to sneak out one night and move the stones a few feet. After all no one would ever know.

There are lots of different ways of stealing. Some seem so small we think they don't matter. (Like managing not to pay on the bus, or taking someone else's pencil or ruler at school or keeping quiet about the peaches the girl forgot to 'ring up' in the shop.) God says that they all matter.

Prayer: *Father, we are faced with lots of opportunities to be dishonest. Help us always to be true to Your standards. Amen.*

June 20   **DEUTERONOMY 19.15–21**

'If anyone gives false witness, claiming he has seen someone do wrong when he hasn't . . . His penalty shall be the punishment he thought the other man would get' (vs.16, 19, Living Bible).

Comment: 'Now then, who wrote that on the blackboard?,' asked Mr. Stevens. 'Richard did, Sir, I saw him,' said Simon. In fact Simon had done it but he is afraid of getting into trouble so he lies and puts the blame on to Richard.

This sort of thing happens everywhere—in shops and schools, in offices and factories. Sometimes we call it 'passing the buck' —when no one will accept responsibility. As Christians when we have done something wrong we should own up. And we should certainly never try to put the blame on someone else by lying.

To think about: What happened to the person who 'gave false witness'? Do you think that would work today?

Prayer: *Lord, please give us the courage to admit our mistakes. Amen.*

June 21   **DEUTERONOMY 34.1–12**

'It is the Promised Land,' the Lord told Moses. 'I have promised Abraham, Isaac and Jacob that I would give it to their descendants. Now you have seen it, but you will not enter it' (v.4, Living Bible).

Comment: Does it seem to you that God has not answered your prayers? Do His promises always seem to work out for you? Sometimes we may feel that God has forgotten and that our prayers are not being answered. But we can be sure that God is working all the time and sometimes we must just be patient. Abraham, Isaac and Jacob died long before their people came to the promised land. Moses died just on the frontier. We are part of something much bigger than ourselves. The answer to our prayers may well be far more wonderful than we could have imagined.

Prayer: *Thank You, Lord, for working in our lives. Please help us to believe this even when we are not sure what You are doing. Amen.*

June 22   **LUKE 9.1–9**

And he called the twelve together . . . and he sent them out (vs. 1, 2, RSV).

Comment: When Christians are planning to do something together, we sometimes find two extremes. The first group plan everything down to the last detail so that there is no room for change to meet particular needs as they arise. The second group may say something like: 'We are relying on the Holy Spirit to tell us what to do' and they plan nothing. Jesus showed a middle way.

Questions: What special job did the disciples have (v.2)? *They knew what they were doing.* What equipment did they have (v.3)? *They knew what not to take.* Where were they to stay (v.4)? What were they to do when they left a city (v.5)? They had some basic rules to follow but room to meet real needs when they came up.

Prayer: *Are there some people in your church who are making plans for something? Pray for them today and the plans that they are making.*

June 23   **LUKE 9.10–17**

And he took them and withdrew apart (v.10, RSV).

Comment: I expect you have special times, and days, and holidays when you like to be alone together and be 'just the family'. Jesus wanted a special time alone with His disciples after their preaching tour but the crowds discovered where He was. When they 'just turned up' He welcomed them and He spent time talking with them and to them. When the disciples advised sending them away because it was a meal time, He suggested that they should all share the food they already had and it became enough for everyone.

Questions: How important do you think it is to be alone as a family from time to time? How do you all behave when someone calls on you when you had hoped to be alone? What do you feel about turning someone away before a meal because you can't afford to entertain them on the family budget?

Prayer: *Lord Jesus, help us to be able to welcome other people in the way You did. Amen.*

'If any man would come after me' (v.23, RSV).
Comment: Tomorrow we'll be thinking about the question Jesus asked in verse 18, but today read verses 23–26 again. If we are following the Lord Jesus, no one of us will be able to think of himself as the most important person in our family, or in the world. Each of us will be prepared to be loyal to God even when it is difficult. We will think 'How much can I give?' rather than 'How much can I get?'; 'What is the right thing to do?' rather than 'What is the easiest?' and 'What is the most I can do?' rather than 'What is the least?'.

The Christian family is the place where we can support and encourage one another to follow Jesus.
Something to do: Share together the ways in which you have found the rest of the family have helped you. Are there any other ways you wish you could help one another in future?
Pray *about them together today.*

'This is my Son, my Chosen; listen to him!' (v.35, RSV).
Comment: Jesus needed to help His disciples discover who He really was. Yesterday we read that He asked them two questions. The first was 'Who do the crowds say that I am?' How did they answer this (v.19)? The second was 'Who do *you* say I am?' How did they answer this (v.20)?

Eight days later, God Himself spoke to them and told them who Jesus, the ordinary man they were used to travelling with day by day, really was. Who was He (v.35)? What were they to do (v.35)?
Question: What are the different ways in which we can listen to Jesus today?
Prayer: *Lord Jesus, today You have reminded us that You are God's Son. Help us to listen to what You wish to say to us as we worship You in church today, and read about You this coming week. Amen.*

'Bring your son here' (v.41, RSV).
Comment: When did your family last get fussed and flustered? What was it all about?

The crowd we've read about today was fussed and flustered.

What about? The problem was taken to Jesus and in His capable hands the fuss and fluster became calm and order. When we next get worked up perhaps we can remind one another to bring the problem to Jesus. He may not offer a miraculous answer as He did then, but thinking through the problem His way may bring the calm and order we need.

Question: Why couldn't the disciples of Jesus help? Is there a clue in verse 41?

Prayer: *Lord Jesus, we so often worry about things and make a fuss. Please help us to remember to bring everything to You so that You are involved in our day to day lives: involved in the way we think, in the things we do and the way we do them. Amen.*

June 27   **LUKE 9.43–48**

But while they were all marvelling at everything he did, he said to his disciples . . . (v.43, RSV).

Comment: As Jesus went about from day to day, He took every opportunity to help the disciples discover who He really was. What new thing did He try to teach them about Himself (v.44)? He also took the opportunity to teach them something about *themselves*. About the way they thought about people and the way they behaved towards others. In those days a child was not a very important person. Read verse 48 again and this time say 'not very important person' instead of child.

Something to remember: A Christian believes that *everyone* matters, and he or she behaves as if they do.

Prayer: *Heavenly Father, please help us to treat everyone we meet today as a person who matters. Amen.*

June 28   **LUKE 9.49–56**

But he turned and rebuked them (v.55, RSV).

Comment: What do you think the word tolerate means? What things do you, as a family, have to tolerate in one another?

James and John were not tolerant. What was John intolerant about (v.49)? Maybe he didn't like the thought that someone else was doing the same sort of thing as they were doing. Maybe it made him feel resentful and jealous. What were James and John upset about (v.53)? They wanted everyone to behave towards Jesus in the way *they* thought they ought to behave.

Think to yourself: Do you ever feel like James and John did? That you would really rather like to punish people for the rude way they talk about Jesus and ignore Him? Jesus does not feel that way. Read again what He said to James and John (v.55).

Prayer: *Lord Jesus, please help us in our own family and in our church family to love one another so much that we are able to tolerate other people who are different from ourselves. Amen.*

June 29   **LUKE 10.1–3; 17–20**

'Go your way; behold, I send you out . . .' (v.3, RSV).

Comment: Is your church having a houseparty, camp, holiday-club or mission soon? What plans have been made? Jesus made careful plans for His mission. He didn't say 'Go where you like, how you like, when you like'. He sent His followers out in couples and carefully gave them instructions telling them where to go and what to do.

After it was over and they got back, they were all very excited because their mission had been a success, but Jesus wanted them to think in a serious way about what had happened. He said, 'The important thing is, not that demons obey you, but that your names are registered as citizens of heaven' (Living Bible).

To think about: It is more important to be excited about what God has done for us than what we do for Him.

Prayer: *Lord Jesus, please help our own church leaders to carefully plan the work You have for us all to do in our own district. Amen.*

June 30   **LUKE 10.25–37**

'Go and do likewise' (v.37, RSV).

Comment: What do you feel like when you see a photograph of a starving child or a battered wife? The interesting thing about the Samaritan was that he allowed himself to *feel* something about the man who had been mugged. The priest *ignored* him, the Levite only *looked*, but the Samaritan *felt*. What did he feel (v.33)? That word 'compassion' means to feel the feelings of another. Because the Samaritan was able to feel like the mugged man felt, he did the best he could for him. Jesus said the Samaritan was the one who really loved his neighbour, and we are to be like him.

Something to do: Next time you meet someone who is ill or unhappy say to yourself 'What is he or she feeling like now?' then 'If he or she feels like that, what would he or she like *me* to do?'

Prayer: *Lord Jesus, thank You for Your compassion and for this story about the Samaritan's compassion. Help us to feel compassion for the people we meet. Amen.*

A woman named Martha received him into her house (v.38, RSV).
Comment: Is your brother or sister like you or different from
you? Martha and Mary were sisters but they were very different
from each other and so they did different things.

Martha was the busy, must-have-a-neat-home-and-entertain-
properly sort of person, so she worried because things were not
right. Mary was the sitting-quietly-and-thinking sort of person
who didn't really notice what had to be done or how worried
Martha was.

God didn't make everyone to be alike, but if Martha and Mary
had understood each other a little better perhaps Martha would
have been sitting down too.

Question: What could Mary have done that she didn't do? What
could Martha have done that she didn't do?

Prayer: *Heavenly Father, please help us to understand one another*
better in our own home and help us to care for one another more.
Amen.

'Lord, teach us to pray' (v.1, RSV).
Comment: Imagine that you have been to the seaside for the day.
You come home tired and sleepy and very late so that all the
family flops into bed. Then, the doorbell rings. 'Go away,' says
Dad, and buries his head in his pillow. But the person does not
go away and the doorbell goes on ringing. In the end the whole
family is awake, so Dad opens the door and lends his next-door
neighbour the spanner he wants to mend his visitor's car.

Jesus is saying that if Dad can be persuaded to open the
front-door just because his neighbour goes on ringing the bell,
how much more will God, who *wants* to hear our prayers and
answer them, and who *wants* to help us, give us what is good for
us.

Remember: 'Everyone who asks receives . . .' (vs.9 and 10).
Prayer: *Read together verses 2, 3 and 4.*

'Nothing is covered up that will not be revealed' (v.2, RSV).
Comment: Who was the last person in your family to take part
in a play? It can be great fun to dress up and act a part when
everyone knows that it is only pretend. Acting is one thing, but

95

pretending to be someone or something we are not in real life is called *hypocrisy*.

The Pharisees were always putting on a good show when people were looking, but they didn't care what they were like in secret. Jesus knew all about them and their pretences. He warned them that they would not be able to deceive people for ever.

Question: In what ways are Christians in danger of being like the Pharisees?

Prayer: *Lord Jesus, we know that You can see us all the time. You know what we are like in secret. Help us to avoid being hypocrites. May we live out in our lives what we believe about You in our hearts. Amen.*

July 4   **LUKE 12.13–21**

A man's life does not consist in the abundance of his possessions (v.15, RSV).

Comment: 'Mum will you get me one of those?' says Tim watching the adverts on television. The mail order catalogue that drops through the door, the TV adverts and the things the neighbours have, all make us want what we have not got. Advertisements are planned to make us think we would be happy if only we had that new kitchen, or camping equipment, or caravan. But they are wrong. These things do not make people happy although happy people can, and often do, enjoy these things if they are fortunate enough to have them.

Question: What should the person who buys lots of things and hoards them up, remember (v.20)?

Keynote: 'Rich toward God' (v.21).

Prayer: *Father God, please forgive us for the times we get caught up in this world's attitudes and find ourselves wanting more and more things. Help us to see the things that matter beyond this earthly world. Amen.*

July 5   **LUKE 12.22–34**

'Don't worry about whether you have enough food to eat or clothes to wear' (v.22, Living Bible).

Comment: It is easy to catch the values and attitudes of the people we live among isn't it? We also want a deep freeze, to bulk buy and to be an agent for mail order fashions. Alison and Terry come home from school saying, 'But Mum, everybody's got new T-shirts, or new shorts, or striped socks, or is getting

96

more pocket-money'—or whatever it is that everybody has got. And we, and they, worry if we are not like everyone else.

Questions: If Dad loses his job and there is not so much money to go round, why shouldn't the Christian family get anxious and upset (v.30)? What did Jesus tell us to look at to remind us that this is so (vs.24, 27)?

Prayer: *Heavenly Father, thank You for providing us with enough food to eat and clothes to wear. Please help us not to let these sort of things matter more than they should. Amen.*

July 6   **LUKE 12.35–40**

'**Be like men who are waiting for their master to come home from the marriage feast, so that they may open to him at once when he comes and knocks**' (v.36, RSV).

Comment: 'Don't worry about how much money you have or haven't got,' said Jesus. 'Don't worry about having enough trendy clothes or eating well but do be ready for God when He comes to you.' Jesus was always helping people to get life in the right perspective, to hold things in the right balance and to know what really matters most.

Something to think about: Are you ready for Jesus to come and teach you what He wants to, when He wants to, or is your mind and life like an attic with too much in it? Maybe work or school take up a lot of time and you have other things to do and to think about. It is possible to be too busy *now* for God to enter and too busy to be ready for Jesus *when He returns*.

Prayer: *Lord Jesus, please help us to get the right balance in our lives so that we are always ready for You to talk to us or to come back to us. Amen.*

July 7   **LUKE 13.10–17**

'**Woman, you are free from your illness**' (v.12, GNB).

Comment: Do you know someone who likes to keep their house so neat and tidy that no one feels at home in it? Or a teacher who cares more about dirty finger-marks on your book than about a good piece of work? Or someone who cares more about what you wear in church than whether you are worshipping God? Jesus taught us not to be petty. When rules and regulations matter more than people, more than their health and well-being and more than their relationship with God, then they have ceased to have any purpose and have become worthless.

Question: How did Jesus show that the ruler of the synagogue's rule was a petty one (v.15)?

Prayer: *Lord God, please help us to understand the difference between helpful rules and regulations and those that make our love for You and for others less real. Amen.*

July 8   **LUKE 13.18–27**

'Struggle to get in through the narrow door' (v.24, NEB).
Comment: An acorn looks a fragile little thing: you can pick it up between your toes or crack it with a small stone. But it hides a secret power that can heave up paving stones, burst walls and make a huge tree. Mustard seeds and leaven have secret power too, and *so does Jesus' Kingdom.* This is going to grow into the most important thing in the world. Nothing can stop it!

'How big will it be?' a Jew asked Jesus. The Jew thought he knew—as big as the Jewish nation, of course, no bigger, no smaller. But Jesus told him simply that the Kingdom is like a house with a narrow door. Everyone must make sure to get inside, himself or herself.

Question: Someone who knows Jesus, and belongs to a Christian family or school Christian Union perhaps, might still be turned away from Christ's Kingdom (v.25). Why is that?
Prayer: *Lord Jesus Christ, help us to obey You because we love You, and so prove that we are Your friends for whom You died. Amen.*

July 9   **LUKE 14.1–6**

'Is it lawful to heal on the sabbath, or not?' (v.3, RSV).
Comment: It never does to pretend that all Christians always think the same way about things, because they don't. The Pharisees had masses of rules about what the Jews must not do on the Sabbath, in the same way as some Christians today believe they should and shouldn't do certain things on Sundays. The way to spend Sunday is something that every family needs to talk about and agree upon together, looking at what the Bible says and thinking out what it means for them, living where they do among their own friends and neighbours. Has your family ever done this? If not, why not do so today?

Two important things to notice from today's reading are:
1. Jesus showed that it is right to help people on the Sabbath.
2. The Pharisees had lost their sense of proportion (v.5).
Prayer: *Creator God, help us to discover the best way to spend the one day of rest You created for us in every seven days. Amen.*

Now he told a parable (v.7, RSV).
Comment: At important dinners, or parties, or at weddings, people stand up and make speeches. Jesus was asked to give the speech at this dinner party. First of all He spoke to the guests. 'Don't ever think of yourself as being an important guest,' He taught them. Then He spoke to His host. 'When you invite people into your home for meals, don't do it just because you hope they'll invite you back.'
Some things to think about: Do you always want the best seat at a party, or a special seat in a committee or at an office function or in the staff-room?

Do you ever invite people to meals who can't have you back, and who won't offer you work or a better business contract?
Prayer: *Heavenly Father, please save us from self-importance and self-interest. Help us always to think of others. Amen.*

'A man once gave a great banquet' (v.16, RSV).
Comment: Most children enjoy parties and no matter what age we are, many of us enjoy coming together in either small or large groups for food and fun. Maybe we enjoy sitting round eating and chatting with just a few friends, or a supper party that takes hours because of the sharing of ideas that goes on. Jesus pictured the Kingdom of God as having this sort of fun and enjoyment about it.
Something to think about: The guests had already accepted the invitation to the banquet, yet when the time came, work mattered more to the first one (v.18), the second got caught up with his latest novelty (v.19) (oxen—but it could equally be a new car), and the third was too involved with one person (v.20). How can these same things keep us out of God's Kingdom today?
Prayer: *Lord God, thank You for reminding us that serving You and being part of Your Kingdom is something we can enjoy. Amen.*

'This man receives sinners and eats with them' (v.2, RSV).
Comment: What were the Pharisees grumbling about in verse 2? There are people today who still think the same sort of way. On the one hand they say, 'We must have a gospel-outreach to the local area' because they wonder why none of the boys and girls

there attend the church, yet they do not allow their own sons and daughters to play out with the local children in case they catch any bad habits. It is no good planning things *for* people who don't come to church if we never mix *with* these people socially, or play with them. The best way to help them is to eat meals with them, play with them or go out with them. Jesus did, but He got criticized for it. So may we if we follow His example.

Question: What makes God and His angels glad (vs.7, 10)?

Prayer: *Heavenly Father, help us as a family to share everything with the people we live among so that we may also share the good news about Jesus with them too. Amen.*

July 13   **LUKE 15.11–24**

'The younger son gathered all he had and took his journey into a far country' (v.13, RSV).

Comment: There are still young people who run away from home and they run, just like this young man did, to the big cities. They find, just like he did, that a lot of money runs out very fast. The young man in this story chose to leave home, but more important, he *chose* to come back. He wasn't sent back by the police or a social worker.

Some young people who run away today really *do* find that their parents don't want them back again. In this story the father had compassion. This means that he was able to feel how his son felt, so he opened his arms and he hugged him to show he was welcome back home.

Something to remember: God allows us to choose whether to go away from Him or whether to come to Him. If we choose to come to Him, He is like the father in the story.

Prayer: *Thank You, God, for having compassion on us and knowing what we feel like. Amen.*

July 14   **LUKE 15.25–32**

But he was angry and refused to go in (v.28, RSV).

Comment: Have you noticed how easy it is for people to be like the older brother? He resented his brother which means he was offended. A girl who is top of the class may not like the new girl because she turns out to be just as clever. A housewife may resent her neighbour who can cook better than she can, or a footballer resent a better player in the team. An older person at church may resent the new person who has come along with some bright ideas so that changes have been made. It is something to watch out for in ourselves when new people arrive at our school, office, church, committee, voluntary organization or in sport.

Something to remember: In God's Kingdom there is no place for resentment. He welcomes everyone who comes to Him.

Prayer: *Heavenly Father, forgive us for the times we have resented other people taking the limelight we might have had. Help us to learn to love and welcome all whom You love and welcome. Amen.*

July 15   LUKE 17.11–19

And he fell on his face at Jesus' feet, giving him thanks (v.16, RSV).

Comment: Auntie Jane gave baby a present and he toddled away with it in his hand, but Mother gently pulled him back and said, 'What do you say to Auntie?' 'Thank you', mutters baby before he toddles off again. We think it is important to teach young children *how* to say thank you, so that when they feel grateful they have words to use to show what they feel. It is also good for the person who has given something to know they are pleased. All the lepers were pleased to be well again but only one bothered to show it.

To think about: If we really care for one another, we shall want people to know when we are grateful. If we really care about what God has done for us, we won't forget to thank Him either —again and again.

Prayer time: *As a family, think of some of the things you are grateful to God for and thank Him together for them now.*

July 16   LUKE 18.9–17

'Two men went up into the temple to pray' (v.10, RSV).

Comment: 'Thank You that we are not like other families. We are a Christian family. We go to church every Sunday and we read the Bible and pray together every day. We are not like other families, money conscious, cheating on our Income Tax returns, getting false expense accounts. We care about our neighbours, about missionaries, about underdeveloped countries and world poverty. Each week we put money in the collection and give to charity.'

It is so easy to slip into thinking this way without realizing what it is we are doing, but if we are like the tax collector in today's story we'll want to consciously pray more like this: O God, we make so many mistakes as we try to live together as a

Christian family, as we try to love You and serve You day by day. Please forgive us and help us to do better. Amen.
Question: How *do* you think of yourselves as a Christian family?
Prayer time: *Pray the prayer above the question or pray together about your answer to the question itself.*

July 17   **LUKE 18.18–30**

'One thing you still lack' (v.22, RSV).
Comment: The rich ruler thought he had obeyed all the commandments but he wanted to be sure that he would have eternal life. Jesus explained that the reason why he was so unsure and unsettled about his future with God, was because he had things that mattered more to him in his present life. The ruler was rich and his riches mattered to him so much that when Jesus encouraged him to share them with other people, he was sad at the thought.
Something to think about: Having things is not necessarily wrong (or sin), but what we do with what we have shows what really matters to us. If you find it difficult to share your home, or your food, or your clothes, or your toys with other people for God's sake, read verses 29 and 30 again.
Prayer: *Heavenly Father, please save us from selfishness. Help us to be able to share the good things You have given us with other people. Amen.*

July 18   **LUKE 18.31–34**

And taking the twelve, he said to them ... (v.31, RSV).
Comment: As we've read Luke's version of Jesus' life we have seen how, when suitable moments came, Jesus tried to help His friends to understand who He was and what was going to happen to Him. Today we've read about Jesus making a special time to carefully explain to them what was soon going to happen. What was it (vs.32, 33)? The sad thing was that His friends couldn't take in what He was saying. They heard Him but they didn't understand.
Something to be ready for: All through our lives Jesus uses certain moments to teach us more about Himself. We can be open and ready to learn.
Prayer: *Lord Jesus, please help each one of us to understand what You try to show us about Yourself from day to day. Amen.*

He enquired what this meant (v.36, RSV).
Comment: Do you know some people who are just like *blobs*?
They never take any interest in anyone or anything. It would
have been so easy for the blind man to have given up trying, to
have lost all interest in living and just sat there like a blob by
the roadside not caring one way or another what happened,
but he didn't. Even though he couldn't see, he still *listened*—
and reacted to what he heard. He *asked questions* and expected
someone to answer. He *screamed for help* and didn't give up till
Jesus had given it to him.
Something to think about: When a person becomes set in his or
her ways, always thinking the same way and doing the same
things, we feel they have grown old too quickly. How 'set' are
you going to let yourself become?
Prayer: *Lord Jesus, help us to remember this blind man and to*
follow his example so that we may go on growing in our minds and
in our relationship with You. Amen.

'Behold, Lord, the half of my goods I give to the poor' (v.8, RSV).
Comment: Think of the person who is the most disliked in your
class at school, the most objectionable in your factory or office,
shop or community. Now, think for a moment what it must feel
like to be that person then you will have some idea of how
Zacchaeus felt. He had done wrong and was hated for it. He
wanted help and was desperate enough to make himself look a
fool finding it.
Question: How did Zacchaeus *show* that although he had previously thought only of himself, he had found a new way of life
by believing the teaching of Jesus (v.8)?
Prayer: *Lord Jesus, please let the things we do be a direct result*
of our love for You and our wish to serve You. Amen.

'Well done, good servant! Because you have been faithful ...'
(v.17, RSV).
Comment: What are the things you are able to do well? In some
families everyone has totally different things they are good at,
in others most members of the family are good at the one thing
—like music, or engineering, or carpentry. Some parents have

skills, some have training and qualifications that bring a lot of money into the home and some don't.

The important thing about the first two servants in today's story is that they each did the best they could do with what they had been given—and the result was different in each case, but the master was equally pleased with them.

Something to think to yourselves about before the prayer: In what ways do you try to do the best you can with the things God made you able to do, and with the money you receive?

Prayer: *Dear God, please help us to use the things You have given us in the best way in Your service. Amen.*

July 22   **LUKE 19.20–26**

'I tell you, that to every one who has will more be given' (v.26, RSV).

Comment: Today we have read about the man who was too careful, too cautious and maybe too lazy. He did not try to do anything with the money he had been given even though he had been told to do so; he just put it away and ignored it. 'Playing safe' it's sometimes called, but the king had trusted him to use the money. He had disobeyed and let the king down.

To think about: God trusts us to use what He has given us and when we do, we'll probably find that in the same way as the good servants did, we'll get given more to do for Him. Our skills and our influence may increase.

Prayer: *Heavenly Father, help us to receive and put to use the gifts You have given us for Your own glory. Amen.*

July 23   **LUKE 19.28–35**

And throwing their garments on the colt they set Jesus upon it (v.35, RSV).

Comment: When we watch a medieval battle at the cinema or on TV we expect to find a royal king riding on a charger. If we're watching a western, we often see warring tribes race by on horses as fast as the wind. In New Testament times, war kings rode on horses, but a king approaching a city in peace rather than for a battle, might well ride on a donkey. Donkeys were not thought of as silly, stubborn, mild pets for children to ride on in the Zoo, they were important, highly thought-of animals.

Something to remember: When Jesus chose to ride on a donkey, He was showing that He was a peaceful king, coming to His people with love.

Prayer: *Lord Jesus, thank You for being our Heavenly King, and especially for being a peaceful and loving one. Amen.*

July 24   LUKE 19.36–40

The whole multitude of the disciples began to rejoice and praise God with a loud voice for all the mighty works that they had seen (v.37, RSV).
Comment: Fun fairs, and festivals and parties are an important highlight in most of our lives. We all need to be able to show our joy and our happiness and our gaiety, for although life can sometimes be serious and sad, parts of it are great fun as well.

Jesus' followers needed to be able to shout and sing and be festive about His leadership and Kingship. Jesus knew this even though the kill-joy Pharisees disapproved. And Jesus still knows it today.
Question: What opportunities do you have in your family and in your local church to have fun together about the joyful parts of the Christian life? Ought there to be more?
Prayer: *Lord Jesus, help us to be able to express the real happiness and joy we feel because You are our Heavenly King. Help us to show it as well as know it. Amen.*

July 25   LUKE 19.41–48

And when he drew near and saw the city he wept over it (v.41, RSV).
Comment: Because Jesus was a real person as well as being God's Son, He had the feelings real people like you and I have. He felt sad when He realized what was going to happen to Jerusalem in the future, when He thought how the rulers wanted power rather than peace. He cried at the thought of it all.

He also cared when He saw injustice. He cared when He saw that ordinary people were being charged far too much for what they were being made to buy in the Temple. He used His anger to do something that brought attention to the matter. What did He do (v.45)?
Question: Think of some injustices that Christians ought to be angry about. Is it enough just to be angry?
Prayer: *Lord Jesus, please help us to react in the genuine, real and helpful way You did as we are faced with many different things happening day by day. Amen.*

What then will the owner of the vineyard do to them? (v.15, RSV).
Comment: 'Will you shut that door?' shouts Dad for the tenth
time. What sorts of things does each member of your family get
fed up with? Picking clothes up off the floor? Leaving the TV
on when you leave the room? Talk about this for a moment now.

The amazing thing about the owner of the vineyard was his
patience. He gave the tenants chance after chance after chance.
However, because they did not change, they finally got what they
deserved. What was this (v.16)?
Question: If God is like the owner of the vineyard and we are
like the tenants, what can we learn about the way God treats us
and the way we ought to treat Him?
Prayer: *Heavenly Father, thank You so much for Your amazing
patience as You deal with us. Amen.*

But he perceived their craftiness (v.23, RSV).
Comment: *Who did the ghost take to the pictures?** Do you know
the answer to this riddle? Riddles can be fun but the riddle
asked by the scribes and chief priests wasn't meant in fun. It
was meant to trap Jesus. What was it (v.22)? The catch was this;
if Jesus said 'No' then they would report Him to the authorities
who would arrest Him. If Jesus said 'Yes' then they would say
He was a false teacher, because the only true King was God and
not Caesar. However He didn't say 'Yes' and He didn't say 'No'.
What did He say (v.25)?
Question: How do you in your own family work out the balance
between putting God first and honouring the state? What things
do you do to show you serve God? What things do you do as a
local citizen?
Prayer: *Heavenly Father, please help us to get the right emphasis
as we play our part as Christian citizens in our own town and
country. Amen.*

* Riddle answer: His ghoul-friend.

He looked up and saw the rich (v.1, RSV).
Comment: The Scribes were 'show-offs' who loved, and expected,
to be made a fuss of in public. In private they were greedy and
cunning.

The widow was quiet and nobody really noticed her. In private she was generous but she suffered a lot because she was so poor. Which sort of person did Jesus condemn (v.47)?
Questions: Think of some people who might be like the scribes today. *How can we avoid becoming like them?*

Think of the people who are like the widow today. *In what ways can we help that sort of person?*
Prayer: *Lord God, help us to care what You think about us and the things we do and don't do, much more than we mind what other people think about us. Amen.*

July 29   **LUKE 22.1–6**

Then Satan entered into Judas called Iscariot (v.3, RSV).
Comment: Judas was an ordinary person and like all ordinary people he had to make choices. Like us, he had to choose when to get up in the morning, what clothes to wear and what to have for breakfast. But we all have to make some choices that are more important than others. We have to choose what to do when we leave school, who to marry, where to live, how many children to have—and these decisions have a lasting effect upon our lives. Judas had to choose whether to support Jesus or whether to let him down, and it was at this point that Judas let Satan control his thinking rather than God.
Something to remember: Satan is still at work in God's world, tempting us to do evil, the opposite of good. Sometimes we have to do a lot of thinking before we make a decision and we need to ask God's help as we think things through.
Prayer: *Dear Heavenly Father, please help us to choose the best way when we have decisions to make. Amen.*

July 30   **LUKE 22.7–13**

'Go and prepare the passover for us, that we may eat it' (v.8' RSV).
Comment: The Passover wasn't the only important thing, the preparations were important too—they were part and parcel of what was going to happen and needed to be done. It's clear that long-term plans had been made about the guest room (v.11) as well as the preparation Peter and John now needed to do.

When you worship God today, remember that once, some Christians made long-term plans to build your church so that you are able to go there today. Now, in 1978, some people keep it clean, put the heat on in winter, arrange flowers and put out hymn-books. These things are an important preparation for the worship that will take place.

Question: What other Christian events in your area need long-term plans and preparations?

Prayer: *Lord God, thank You for everyone who has played a part in preparing our church for our worship service today, and for the Sunday School and Bible Classes. Amen.*

July 31   LUKE 22.14–23

And he took a cup ... And he took bread (vs.17, 19, RSV).
Comment: 'I'm sorry, I forgot!' How often do you find yourselves having to say this? We all get so busy with what we are playing or what we are doing, that we forget things, sometimes even important things.

The Lord Jesus knew how easy it is for people to be so busy that they forget things, even important things. He also understood how much easier it is to remember something we've seen and taken part in than something we've only been told.

Questions: What two things did the disciples *see* (vs.17, 19)? What would they remember seeing Jesus do with these things?

These two things still take place among Christians today to help us remember Jesus, who He was and what He did. When and how do they happen in your church?

Prayer: *Lord Jesus, thank You for giving us a pattern for the meal that still helps us all to remember You. Amen.*

August 1   LUKE 22.24–30

'But not so with you; rather let the greatest among you become as the youngest, and the leader as one who serves' (v.26, RSV).
Comment: At most birthday parties who usually sits at the top of the table? At a wedding, where do the bride and bridegroom usually sit?

Jesus often asks Christians to think in a different way from the way the rest of the world thinks about things. The world thinks that important people matter more than ordinary people. Our newspapers are full of stories about the kinds of people the world thinks important enough to be 'top people'.

The disciples wanted to be the most important people in Jesus' Kingdom, but Jesus taught them that it was more important to follow His example. What was this (v.27)?

Question: In what ways can you as a family serve other people?

Prayer: *Lord Jesus, please help us as we try to follow Your example and serve other people. Amen.*

'I have prayed for you that your faith may not fail; and when you have turned again, strengthen your brethren' (v.32, RSV).
Comment: 'I'll swim five lengths,' said Peter, 'I won't get tired.' On the day of the swimming gala, Peter was so excited that he was exhausted after four lengths and had to stop.

Simon Peter was like him; he was very sure that he wouldn't let Jesus down, no matter what happened. Yet Jesus knew better. Simon Peter meant well and he loved Jesus a lot, but he was *too* sure of himself. He was to find out that he wasn't as brave as he thought he was, but after that, what *would* he be able to do (v.32)?
Something to remember: We don't fail *so that* we can help other people, but when we do fail, we can help other people so that they need not make the same mistakes.
Prayer: *Lord Jesus, please help us when we are weak so that we don't let You down. Amen.*

'. . . nevertheless not my will, but thine, be done' (v.42, RSV).
Comment: When did you last try to wriggle out of doing something you didn't really want to do? Jesus knows what it feels like and much more. Jesus went through very real agonies when He thought about dying on the cross. He was fighting with being afraid and trying to come to terms with it. He asked God for two things:

1. That if possible He wouldn't have to go through with it.

2. That nevertheless if it was God's best plan then it would happen.

Even though Jesus' earthly friends let Him down and didn't give Him the support He needed in His struggle at this time, what *did* happen (v.43)?
Question: Can you think of anyone you know who, this week, has something very difficult to do; something he or she would rather run away from but who knows that God wishes him or her to go on?
Pray *for them now.*

While he was still speaking, there came a crowd (v.47, RSV).
Comment: What did Judas do (v.47)? How do you think *he* felt?
What did the followers of Jesus ask (v.49)? How do you think *they* felt?

What had the chief priests come to do? How do you think *they* felt?

Judas was the odd man out, the man who was playing a part. He was the one who was pretending to say 'Hello' to his friend when he was really feeling and doing something quite different. **Question:** Can you think of any occasions when you might be tempted to play a part and when you would be letting Jesus down by doing so?

Prayer: *Lord Jesus, we don't really want to let You down by our behaviour, but sometimes we find it hard when we know that other people do not share our love for You. Help us not to pretend that we are one thing when really we are another. Amen.*

August 5   **LUKE 22.54–62**

'Certainly this man was also with him' (v.59, RSV).

Comment: We mustn't be too hard on Peter. He was, after all, a *brave* man. Instead of hiding or running away he went to the high priest's house and became one of the crowd. It was being there that got him into difficulties. He found that when the crunch came, he wasn't brave enough to admit that he was one of Jesus' men.

Today some Christians are brave enough to go to countries where things are difficult, and some find themselves in very difficult situations in their *own* country. Who does your family know in this position? We need to pray for people like this so that when the situations they face are especially difficult, they will have the strength not to let Jesus down.

Prayer: *Lord Jesus, please help all Christians who are in difficult situations today. Encourage them so that they have the strength they need, especially . . . (mention the people you know here). Amen.*

August 6   **LUKE 22.63–71**

And they spoke many other words against him, reviling him (v.65, RSV).

Comment: Perhaps *you* have been made fun of at school or at work and you know how hard it is to be the odd man out. If you've been made fun of and been jeered at, you know what it feels like. Jesus knows exactly what it feels like, too. Read verses 63–65 again.

Jesus did not get a fair trial from the council. He knew that if He told the truth, they wouldn't believe Him, and they didn't.

They chose to accuse Him of the crime of blasphemy; of claiming to be God when He wasn't. We know that *He* was, but they weren't prepared to accept that.

Think now: Do you know anyone who is feeling isolated and left out? Someone who has moved away from home? Someone who is lonely? Someone who is being *made* to feel left out by others? **Pray** *for them today.*

August 7   LUKE 23.1–5

And they began to accuse him (v.2, RSV).

Comment: Think back to yesterday's reading. Of what crime did the priests and Scribes accuse Jesus? This put them in a difficult situation themselves. They were not allowed to give the death sentence, it had to be given by a Roman governor. They knew that Pilate would think their accusation just a petty religious squabble, so what three things did they now accuse Jesus of doing (v.2)?

To think about: They changed their tune to suit their own circumstances and what they wanted. Perhaps you have met some people like them. By contrast, Christians stand for truth.

Prayer: *Lord Jesus, please help all Christian lawyers and politicians, all who sit on public committees and have important statements to make today. Help them to speak truthfully without distorting the facts. Amen.*

August 8   LUKE 23.6–17

Nothing deserving death has been done by him (v.15, RSV).

Comment: Learning to decide things wisely is an important part of growing up and being mature. As children we learn to say 'yes' and 'no' to small things, then as we grow older, our parents let us make decisions about more important things so that we gradually learn to choose sensibly.

Herod was not prepared to make a decision about Jesus, he just sent Him back to Pilate. But Pilate made *his* decision. He did not believe Jesus was guilty of the charges brought against Him. What did he suggest should be done (v.16)?

Something to talk about: How much learning about decision-making is each member of your family allowed? What things does each member have the right to say 'yes' and 'no' to?

Prayer: *Heavenly Father, help each one of us to go on discovering how to make wise, careful decisions based on true facts. Amen.*

So Pilate gave sentence that their demand should be granted (v.24, RSV).

Comment: Last Sunday we thought how difficult it is to be the odd man out and how awful it can feel. Jesus had the strength to put up with it because of what He knew and believed about God. Pilate was different. He knew that Jesus wasn't guilty and he didn't want to kill Him, but he hadn't the strength to be the odd man out and stand against the crowd. It was difficult for Pilate because he knew that if there was an uproar, he might be reported to Rome and lose his job. What did he do (v.25)?

To think over: It is far easier to give in to those who are wrong than to stand for what we know to be right. We need God's strength as Jesus did.

Prayer: *Heavenly Father, please give us Your strength today to be true to what we know and believe about You. If we are tempted to join the crowd help us to remember what we have read in Your Word. Amen.*

'Father, forgive them' (v.34, RSV).

Comment: Imagine that you have been thrown into prison as a political prisoner and the guards torture you. How do you think you would feel about those guards the next time you saw them? How do you think you would feel about your friends if they had all run away and left you to be tortured? Read verse 34 again. Even though Jesus had been left to be the odd man out, even though He had been laughed at, beaten and tortured, He was not angry. Nor was He resentful. He did not hate the people who had done all this to Him, He loved them so much that He asked God to forgive them. This was what He wanted and what He still wants.

Question: Do you think it is possible for us to love like that?

Prayer: *Heavenly Father, please help us to learn to love other human beings as much as Jesus did, no matter what they do to us. Amen.*

'Do you not fear God, since you are under the same sentence of condemnation?' (v.40, RSV).

Comment: Have you ever heard an old man or an old woman

say, 'I'm too old. I can't change now'? One of the things we can learn from today's reading is that it is never too late to turn to Jesus. For both the men we've read about it was the last moment in their lives.

What did the first criminal say (v.39)?

What did the second one say (v.42)?

How did Jesus reply (v.43)?

Question: Are there some older members of your family who have not yet become Christians? If so, remember to go on praying for them.

Prayer: *Heavenly Father, thank You that we can come to You at all times and in all places. May all Christians who visit men and women in prisons help the people there to understand that they can turn to You in spite of what they have done. Amen.*

August 12   **LUKE 23.44–49**

The curtain of the temple was torn in two (v.45, RSV).

Comment: If you have ever visited a stately home, or a museum, or a big cathedral, you will probably have come across a door, screen or curtain shutting off part of the building with a notice to say that you are not allowed to go through there.

The curtain in the Temple was like a great big room divider. No one except the high priest was allowed to go through into the holy of holies, and even he was allowed through only once a year. What happened to this curtain when Jesus died (v.45)?

It was just as if God was showing the world that the way to God was now open for everyone to go through.

Question: What good thing can we learn about death from the words Jesus said as He died (v.46)?

Prayer: *Heavenly Father, thank You that because Jesus died, the way to You is now open for everyone who wishes to come to You. Thank You for receiving us when we ask You to do so both in this life and when we die. Amen.*

August 13   **LUKE 23.50–56**

He was a member of the council, a good and righteous man (v.50, RSV).

Comment: How do you treat your friends *after* they've been punished at school, or *after* they've been in hospital, or even after they've served a prison sentence? Joseph had been interested in Jesus when He was alive, so after He died, instead of leaving the body to rot on the hill-side like any other criminal's body, what did Joseph do (vs.52,53)? What did the women do (v.56)? Joseph behaved as he did because of the sort of person he was. What was that (v.50)?

Think spot: Can you as a family think of anyone you should be showing more care to at this time because of the sort of people you claim to be as Christians? Is there anything you can do for them *today*?

Prayer: *Help us, Heavenly Father, to follow Joseph's example and show by our actions that we care for the family and friends You have given to us. Amen.*

August 14   **LUKE 24.1–12**

At early dawn, they went to the tomb (v.1, RSV).

Comment: You know the excitement that there is when your favourite team has won the football match. Imagine racing into the kitchen to tell Mum the news and she turns round and tells you she doesn't believe you. What would you feel like? How could you convince her, now that the match is over and it wasn't televised, that your team really had won?

What exciting news did the two Marys bring (v.7)?

What did the rest of the apostles think (v.11)?

The news was just too staggering for them to be able to believe it.

Prayer: *We pray for all those who find it hard to believe the good news about Jesus Christ; who find it hard to believe that He really rose from the dead and is alive today. Heavenly Father, please help them to understand. Amen.*

August 15   **LUKE 24.13–27**

Jesus himself drew near and went with them (v.15, RSV).

Comment: When someone in the family has been very ill, or loses her job, or has a car accident, we sometimes hear people say, 'Why did God allow this to happen?' or 'It just doesn't make sense'.

What had happened to Jesus just didn't make sense to His friends. Two of them were talking about it and trying to puzzle it out as they walked down the road together. When Jesus came and joined them, He was able to help them understand it all— even though they didn't realize who He was.

Something to think about: Do you remember to ask Jesus to help you to understand the things that God allows to happen to your own family and friends?

Prayer: *Lord Jesus, please help us to understand why You allow puzzling things to happen in our lives. Amen.*

August 16 LUKE 24.28–35

And their eyes were opened and they recognized him (v.31, RSV).
Comment: When something very exciting happens at school, you rush home and say, 'Mum I must tell you something!' It's not much fun if you haven't got someone to share your excitement, is it?

When the two travellers arrived in their home village they invited Jesus back to supper, to share their own meal in an ordinary home. It was only as Jesus shared their own bread and gave thanks for it, doing it the same way as He had always done it, that they both recognized who He really was. They were so excited. What did they do there and then (vs.33–35)?

Something to think about: Does the truth about the Lord Jesus still excite you so much that you want to share it with others?

Prayer: *Lord Jesus, help us once again to feel the excitement of the discovery that You are still alive. Help us to share this news with others. Amen.*

August 17 LUKE 24.36–43

But they were startled and frightened (v.37, RSV).
Comment: What kinds of things frighten you? Some people can't bear spiders; others don't like the dark; some are scared of heights or thunder and lightning. Some are afraid of God! In the Bible God has shown us that He never wishes any one of His servants to be frightened of Him or of the Lord Jesus. You will notice that every time He sent an angel messenger to this world, the first words the angel said were, 'Don't be afraid'.

The disciples were frightened when they saw Jesus but straightaway He said and did things to get rid of their fear.

What did He say (v.38)?

What did He do (v.39)?

He had risen from the dead but they need not be afraid of Him.

Something to note: 'The fear of the Lord' does not mean we are to be afraid of God, but it means we are to respect Him.

Prayer: *Lord Jesus, thank You that we can know You as a friend and that we need never be afraid of You. Amen.*

Then he opened their minds to understand the scriptures (v.45, RSV).

Comment: Have you ever had one of those tricky maths problems that you can't work out, or puzzled over a difficult knitting pattern or grappled with an Income Tax form? What a relief when someone comes along and explains it so that your mind can grasp it. What a relief for the disciples when Jesus explained what the Scriptures had been saying about His death and His coming back to life again so that God could forgive people for the things they had done wrong. What a relief both for them and for us to understand, at last, what it was all about.

Question: What happened after Jesus had explained everything to the disciples (v.51)?

Prayer: *Lord Jesus, we thank You for the people You use to explain the Bible to us today so that we may understand it better. Please help them in their work and speak to us through what they are doing. Amen.*

Jesus foretold that Jerusalem would be destroyed—and so it was by the Roman army in AD 70. This was not the first time. In 586 BC Nebuchadnezzar's forces had captured the city, burned it and taken many of the Jews off to Babylon as prisoners. God, however, didn't forget His people. In the Book of Ezra which we begin today, and in Nehemiah (to be read next month), we discover how God enabled His people to return and rebuild their city and its Temple. Between these two books we read a letter written to Christian Jews—Hebrews.

The Lord stirred up the spirit of Cyrus, king of Persia (v.1, RSV).

Comment: Do you ever wake up in the morning with a great desire to do some job that you've been putting off for ages? Perhaps it's visiting a sick friend; writing a letter to say 'thank you' for something or even just being more helpful and unselfish at home. And at the end of the day, do you sometimes crawl into bed without having done a thing about it?

King Cyrus got up one morning determined to get things started on building a house for God in Jerusalem, and by the time he went to bed he had changed the lives of thousands of people. God was working in his heart.

The story of Ezra will show us what can happen when a man—

even a king—obeys God. God can speak to kings and queens and He can speak to us, however young or unimportant we may be.
Question: Am I listening for God?
Prayer: *Please put Your desires into our hearts as we start out each day, Lord, and help us to obey what You say to us. Amen.*

August 20   **EZRA 1.5–11**

And all who were about them aided them (v.6, RSV).
Comment: Seventy years is a very long time and many of the Jews who had been captured were too old to go back to Jerusalem. Only their children and grandchildren could actually go back, but the old people could help (v.6).

The younger Jews were going to clear up the mess that had been left in Jerusalem when their parents and grandparents had been captured, and they were going to rebuild the house of the Lord. The old folks helped by providing what was needed. Animals were needed to carry provisions, and pots and pans for cooking as well as valuables for trading. It was not going to be easy living amongst ruins until some kind of housing could be built.
Question: Can we learn anything from this story about ways in which we can *all* help others in our home, our church and on the mission field?
Prayer: *Lord God, there is a lot of work to be done for You. Show us what part we can play and give us a mind to do it, for Your name's sake. Amen.*

August 21   **EZRA 3.1–7**

The people gathered as one man to Jerusalem (v.1, RSV).
Comment: After the Sunday morning service, a lady was trying to gather her husband and her three children together to go home. She said, 'I can get one or two of them together, but when I go to find the others and come back, I find I've lost the first ones again!' Is it like that in your family sometimes, perhaps at mealtimes or bedtime?

The people who had gone back to Israel were very excited to see their own town or village and eager to make a start on finding somewhere to live, but they had come back for something far more important than that, and so they all came to Jerusalem 'as one man'. It was a united effort when they set up the altar and began to worship God in the way that He had laid down for them.

117

Question: Have you noticed how much quicker and happier it is when we do something together, rather than all pulling in different directions?

Prayer: *Heavenly Father, forgive us when we allow less important things to hinder us from worshipping You. Help us to put You first. Amen.*

'For he is good, for his steadfast love endures for ever toward Israel' (v.11, RSV).

Comment: The Temple was a long way from being finished, but the laying of the foundation was something to be happy about. God had been good to the Israelites in the past. He was showing His goodness to them now, and they could be quite sure that His love for them would go on for ever. So they wrote a special song about it to mark the occasion when the foundation had been completed. It was a good beginning.

Not many new churches and chapels are built in these days, but when it does happen, there is usually a ceremony to mark the laying of the foundation stone. If you look at your church you will probably find this stone with the date and the name of the person who laid it.

A good foundation is very important for a building and also for a person's life.

To think about: Read Luke 6.47–49.

Prayer: *Thank You, Lord, for Your goodness which goes on and on. May we build our lives upon the foundation of Jesus as Saviour and then we know that we can always have a song in our hearts. Amen.*

Then the people of the land discouraged the people of Judah, and made them afraid to build (v.4, RSV).

Comment: Bill was painting a poster at school. Another boy picked up a brush and said, 'Let me help you, Bill'. 'No,' said Bill, 'it's got to be my own work for a competition.' The other boy made such a nuisance of himself that Bill was afraid to go on in case his poster was spoiled.

The enemies of the Israelites first of all tried to spoil the building whilst pretending to help. When that didn't work, they began to be a nuisance, telling tales and lies to king Cyrus, hoping that the king would stop the work going on. Look how long they kept this up (vs.5,6).

Wherever there is work going on for God, Satan sees to it that someone tries to hinder or spoil it. They may appear to want to help but we soon see that they are out to make trouble (see 2 Corinthians 11.13–15).

To think over: Choosing friends and helpers can be very difficult. How do we choose them (Amos 3.3)?

Prayer: *Lord Jesus, we thank You for being our friend and helper. Help us to choose earthly friends carefully. Amen.*

August 24   **EZRA 4.11–16**

'You will find in the book of the records . . .' (v.15, RSV).

Comment: When a prisoner comes out of prison having served his sentence, he often finds it very difficult to live a normal life again because people remember what he did. We read stories in newspapers or hear them over the radio which show that someone has been searching old records to find out the bad things that a person may have done in the past. Our failures are often the things that others remember about us, and it is hard to make a new beginning.

The Jews in Jerusalem had been rebellious in the past and their enemies were not going to let them or the king forget it.

To think about: God knows all about our failures. What does He do about them when we trust in Him and make a new beginning? (See Acts 3.19; Psalm 103.12; Hebrews 8.12.)

Prayer: *Thank You, Heavenly Father, for being willing to forgive and forget when we come to You and trust in You. Help us to treat others as You treat us. Amen.*

August 25   **EZRA 4.17–24**

Then the work on the house of God which is in Jerusalem stopped (v.24, RSV).

Comment: Have you ever looked forward to something very much—perhaps an outing or a party—and then, for some reason, you were not able to go? It is hard to bear disappointments like that and we wonder why it has been allowed to happen to us.

The letter from the king must have been a bitter blow. It seemed to the Israelites that their enemies had won and that evil had overcome good.

If you ever feel like that, take courage today (Psalm 92.7). The building stopped because of the enemies of Israel—everyone could see that. But God had not stopped His work—the enemies couldn't see that, and for a while God's people couldn't either. As we read on, we shall see just how busy God was.

Think spot: God *never* stops working in the world. He never sleeps (Psalm 121.3–4).

Prayer: *We praise You, Lord God, that You are always working in our world. Help us to remember this when we are faced with disappointments. Amen.*

August 26   **EZRA 5.6–13,17**

'We are the servants of the God of heaven and earth' (v.11, RSV).
Comment: 'Who told you that you could do it?' asked the king's governor. The Jews could have replied, 'King Cyrus', which was quite true, and that would probably have avoided awkward questions. But they had had a command from Someone higher than the king and they must mention His name first. They were obeying God, who had given even King Cyrus his orders.

It is hard to tell others about Jesus who came to die for us so that our sins could be forgiven. When Sue was asked what she learned at Girls' Brigade, she replied, 'Oh, we make models, and march, and sing, and do projects and things like that'. It was perfectly true, but it was not the most important thing she learned at Girls' Brigade.

Question: What does today's reading say to us as a family?

Prayer: *Heavenly Father, we want to obey what You say in all that we do. Give us the strength to stand up for You when we have the opportunity. Amen.*

August 27   **EZRA 6.1–5**

Concerning the house of God at Jerusalem, let the house be rebuilt (v.3, RSV).
Comment: Two days ago we thought about the problem of evil appearing to overcome good. But God had been silently working even though the building had stopped. The enemies of the Jews had asked for the records to be searched (4.15), and so they were, but two can play at that game. The records showed that King Cyrus had commanded God's house to be built. They also showed that the building had to be paid for from the King's treasury— which was the bit that had been forgotten. So what had looked like a dreadful setback when the work stopped, now turned out to be a good thing. Not only could the building go on, but it was

120

going to be paid for by the very person whom the enemies had thought would stop the work altogether!

Think spot: When God allows disappointments, He usually has something much better in mind for us.

Prayer: *Lord God, we are glad that we can trust You to work things out for the best for us. Amen.*

August 28   EZRA 6.6–12

'Pray for the life of the king and his sons' (v.10, RSV).

Comment: Perhaps it was what he read in the reports that made King Darius think about God. He must have realized that God was great and powerful or he would not have asked the Jews to pray for him and his sons.

The Bible tells us to pray for our rulers (1 Timothy 2.1–3). They may be Christians or non-Christians, but they all need wisdom from God to do their work properly. In Britain, the Sovereign is the guardian of the Christian faith and it must often be difficult for her to know what decisions to make. That is why our prayers are so important. Then there are the members of the government who plan things that affect us all. God cares about our world and the way the countries live and work together. Let us ask Him to use His power to help those who govern, even though they may not realize where the help is coming from.

Question: Do we really believe that prayer can change things?

Prayer: *Thank You, Lord God, for listening to us when we pray. Give Your wisdom to all who rule over us, and may they grow to love and serve You for themselves. Amen.*

August 29   EZRA 6.13–18

And the people of Israel . . . celebrated the dedication of this house of God with joy (v.16, RSV).

Comment: What a wonderful new beginning! The past rebellion and captivity in Babylon was over. The Israelites were back home and God had given them a fresh start. No wonder they were full of joy and wanted to serve Him in the Temple in the way that God had told them.

This is similar to what happens to us when we repent and trust the Lord Jesus as Saviour. Past sins are forgiven and forgotten (as we saw on August 24th). A completely new life lies ahead, with opportunities of serving God. Satan will try to hinder us just as the enemies tried to stop the Jews from building, but God is able to bring us through.

Think spot: Our lives can be built like the Temple we have been reading about. See Ephesians 2.19–22.

Prayer: *We want You to build our lives, Lord God, making them strong and good through Jesus our Saviour. Help us to make this new beginning. Amen.*

August 30   **HEBREWS 1.1–9**

Thus he became far greater than the angels (v.4, Living Bible).

Comment: The Jewish people (to whom this letter was written) had a very high regard for angels. The writer of the letter wanted them to understand that the Lord Jesus Christ was far more important than any angel. All that Jesus did bore the 'stamp' (or 'mark') of the authority of God. Jesus came to show us what God was like.

Question: Do your actions and attitudes 'mark' you out as a follower of Jesus Christ? Do people who come into your home recognize it as a Christian one?

Prayer: *Dear Lord Jesus, we are often bad tempered, selfish, lazy, unforgiving and rude. At such times we know we are not like You, and are unworthy of being called Your followers. Please forgive us, and fill us with Your love and power. Amen.*

August 31   **HEBREWS 2.1–4**

So we must listen very carefully to the truths we have heard or we may drift away from them (v.1, Living Bible).

Comment: If you just sit in a boat on the river, without making any attempt to row it, you will soon find that you are drifting. You may not *mean* to go in that direction, but you have not done anything to prevent it.

Christian families can drift along without making any real progress unless they know exactly where they are heading, and are all making a real effort to get there.

To discuss together: What are your aims as a family?

Prayer: *Lord Jesus Christ, thank You for offering us the gift of Your wonderful life that never ends. Help us to keep our eyes on the goal You have set for us and to serve You faithfully today and always. Amen.*

Consider Jesus ... He was faithful to him who appointed him (vs.1, 2, RSV).
Comment: When a man and a woman get married, the place where they live becomes their home; *they* create it. All the people who live in that home become a household. In some households the boys and girls have jobs to do as well as the adults. Who has special jobs to do in your household? Are they done well or not?

In God's household, *Moses* was a servant who did what he had to do, well. In God's household, *Jesus* was the Son who did everything loyally. He never, ever, let God down. If we are people who love God and obey Him, we are part of His household, too.
Thinking point: What kind of a member of God's household are you at the moment?
Prayer: *Heavenly Father, help us to discover how we can all be better members of Your household. Amen.*

But Jesus the Son of God is our great high priest (v.14, Living Bible).
Comment: The most important person in the Jewish Temple Services was the high priest. It was his job to accept gifts made by people who knew they had done wrong, and offer them to God as a way of saying 'sorry'.

The writer of this letter is trying to explain to the Jewish people that things have now changed. They no longer need high priests to offer 'sorry' presents—Jesus is their great high priest and He has offered to God the only 'sorry' present that anyone will ever need, and the only one that God will accept—the gift of Jesus' own life.
Prayer: *Lord Jesus, we know You understand all our temptations and weaknesses because You were faced with the same problems when You were here on earth. Please deal gently with us, and forgive us, because we know You died for this purpose. Amen.*

But Jesus lives for ever and continues to be a Priest so that no one else is needed (v.24, Living Bible).
Comment: Whenever we appoint a Pastor, Churchwarden, Sunday School Superintendent or C.U. Secretary it soon becomes

obvious that the person chosen (although we expect them to be much better than we are) often turns out to be just as bad as the rest of us. We seem to be continually putting new people up for election, too, either because of old age, ill-health or moving house. The Jewish people had similar problems with the appointment of Temple priests.

With Jesus as high priest all this is changed, because He lived a perfect life and so is much, much better than we are. He lives for ever, too, so we shall not need someone else to take His place.
Prayer: *Dear Father in heaven, thank You for sending Jesus to this world; thank You for His perfect life and for the fact that He lives for ever. We worship You because we know that this makes it possible for us to come to You. Amen.*

September 4   HEBREWS 8.7-13

For the old one (agreement) is out of date now, and has been put aside for ever (v.13, Living Bible).
A driving licence, insurance policy, TV or dog licence that is out of date is absolutely worthless. Jewish people tried very hard to keep the many written laws which told them what they could or could not do, but they found they could never quite manage it. Now they were out of date, Jesus had introduced one up-to-date and simple law that would replace all the old ones. It is sometimes called a 'law of love' because it is based on our love for Jesus. Because we love Him we obey Him—and we love other people, too, and want to help them.
Think: Is this the up-to-date law of your home and family? When there is washing-up to be done, or leaves to be swept up, or a parcel to be wrapped or an errand to run do you keep this law?
Prayer: *Dear Lord Jesus, please put Your new law of love in all our hearts so that we will WANT to obey You, and help us to show our love for You by loving and serving other people, particularly those within our own family circle. Amen.*

September 5   HEBREWS 9.1-10; 24-26

Christ has entered, not into a sanctuary made with hands ... but into heaven itself, now to appear in the presence of God on our behalf (v.24, RSV).
Comment: It would be interesting to see if any of your family could draw the tent described today. The people who went there to worship God found it very beautiful inside. To them every piece of furniture had a meaning. The high priest was the only

person allowed to go into the inner tent, and he went in only once every year. That was a special day. He would offer sacrifices and pray that God would forgive all the people.

The Lord Jesus is now able to do much more. He is in heaven itself. He faces God Himself and talks about us and for us. And He is there because His sacrifice for our sins doesn't have to be repeated.

Prayer: *Thank You, God, that nowadays we do not need to depend upon any human as a go-between between us and Yourself. Thank You that we can know You as our Father because we believe in Jesus. Amen.*

September 6   HEBREWS 10.26-31

Think how much more terrible the punishment will be for those who have trampled underfoot the Son of God (v.29, Living Bible).
Comment: How would Mum feel if, when she had carefully ironed a shirt or blouse for one of your family she found it left in a heap on the floor? When you have spent time and trouble over something, it is very disappointing to see it 'trampled underfoot' by people who don't care.

God has offered to all of us the free gift of forgiveness for our sins, and life that will go on for ever. If we insult Him by refusing His gift, and treating the fact that Jesus gave His life for us as unimportant—then we surely deserve that God should lose patience with us.

Prayer: *Dear Father God, You have offered us, through the Bible, the gift of forgiveness and everlasting life. Help each one of us to accept Your gift with grateful and thankful hearts. For Jesus' sake. Amen.*

September 7   HEBREWS 11.1-4

(Faith) is the certainty that what we hope for is waiting for us, even though we cannot see it ahead (v.1, Living Bible).
Comment: My dog knows I will feed her at four o'clock each day and she follows me into the kitchen, wagging her tail even though she cannot see the food.

Abel did not understand why God told him to bring Him a lamb for a present but he obeyed God nevertheless even though he couldn't see any reward ahead. Obeying God, even when we do not really understand why, and can see no reward in view for doing so, shows that we have faith in Him.

Do you trust your parents enough to obey them, even when

you do not understand *why* you cannot do what you want to do, or go where you want to go, and can see no particular advantage in being obedient? That is how God wants us to obey Him.

Prayer: *Lord, give us as a family, the kind of faith that is prepared to obey You because we trust You, even when we cannot see clearly what lies ahead. Amen.*

September 8   **HEBREWS 11.7-10**

Noah's belief in God was in direct contrast to the sin and disbelief of the rest of the world (v.7, Living Bible).

Comment: Noah believed and trusted God enough to build a strong houseboat where he and his family could shelter from the storm and flood. Abraham believed and trusted God enough to leave his home and travel through the desert land living in a tent.

God expects your family to believe and trust in Him in quite different ways and circumstances from other families who may also go to your church.

Some families do not believe and trust in God at all. God wants the belief and trust of His people to be a complete contrast to the sin and disbelief of the rest of the world.

Talking point: In what way is God expecting your family to believe and trust Him just now? Is it about moving house, illness, trouble with Granny, Dad's job, or difficulties in your church?

Prayer: *Lord Jesus, You know the special things about which our family needs to believe and trust just now (especially about . . .). We pray for families whom we know who do not believe and trust in You at all. Help them to see our faith, and want to share it. Amen.*

September 9   **HEBREWS 11.13-16**

They were just strangers visiting down here (v.13, Living Bible).

Comment: When a family takes over a caravan or chalet for the holidays (or goes camping) there are often quite a few things that they learn to do without. Mum may use a milk bottle instead of a rolling pin, or a fork instead of a beater, because she knows that she is 'just visiting' and it is not her real home.

Sometimes we forget we are supposed to be 'just visiting' here on earth, and that this is not our permanent and only home. We think and care so much about the good things of *this* life that we forget we should be 'living for heaven'. True men of faith do not make this mistake.

126

Think spot: How many things in your home could you 'do without' without making it less comfortable? If you disposed of these things would it provide money for someone with much greater needs than yours, and also relieve you from the unnecessary chore of cleaning and caring for the 'extras'?

Prayer: *Dear Father in Heaven, we confess that we are all guilty of continually wanting things that are of no real or lasting value. Help us to live in a way that will prepare us for our permanent heavenly home. Amen.*

September 10   **HEBREWS 12.1–3**

Let us strip off anything that slows us down or holds us back (v.1, Living Bible).

Comment: Some boys and girls do their best school work when their teacher is standing over them and watching them. Some Mums only bake especially good cakes if someone is coming to tea. Some Dads are more patient with their children in public than they are in private.

Football supporters expect their favourite team to play well all the time—regardless of the size of the crowd. We have a 'huge crowd of men of faith watching us from the grandstands' as we run the 'race' of the Christian life. That is why we are 'on show' even when we think we are alone, as well as when we are in public. We need to strip off anything that is getting in the way (you don't see Olympic runners racing in overcoats do you?) and keep our eyes on Jesus our 'leader and instructor' so that we run a good race.

Think spot: Could any of these things hinder us in the race of life: watching too much TV; buying too many clothes or sweets; reading the wrong kind of books?

Prayer: *Dear Father, we pray for fit and energetic bodies, clean and wise minds, and active and strong spirits, so that we may run the race of life with patience and perseverance. Amen.*

September 11   **HEBREWS 12.7–11**

Whoever heard of a son who was never corrected? (v.7, Living Bible).

Comment: How many spoiled children do you know? They are usually fussy over their food, rude to their parents, spiteful to their schoolfriends, cheeky to their teachers and sulky if they cannot have their own way. I expect Mum and Dad would say about such children: 'It is their *parents'* fault'.

God (our heavenly Father) knows that if He does not train us we shall grow up like spoiled children. We do not always like being trained, and we certainly do not enjoy being punished, but we need to remember that God's correction is always 'for our good'.

To talk over together: God doesn't slap us, send us to our rooms, stop our pocket money or make us wipe up the muddy footprints that we have made across the kitchen floor. In what ways *does* He correct and punish us?

Prayer: *Lord, we have so much to learn about the kind of life that You want us to live, and the way in which we should treat other people, and how to get to know You better. Give us ears that are prepared to listen and wills that want to obey. Amen.*

September 12   HEBREWS 12.12–15

Try to stay out of all quarrels ... Look after each other (vs. 14, 15, Living Bible).

Comment: See if each member of your family can follow this advice today and compare notes tomorrow to see how successful you have been. Here are some suggestions, but you will be able to think of many other practical ways of carrying it out:

1. At school—don't quarrel over who gets the best pencil, who is the leader in P.E. or games, or who goes first in the dinner queue. Keep your eye open for the shy new girl or the boy whose Mum is ill.

2. Mum—watch out for that awkward neighbour, the cheeky shop assistant and the church gossip, but try to fit in a visit to an old lady, or a friend in hospital.

3. Dad—beware of the newly promoted 'know all', the slap-dash typist, and your reaction if you can't find a clean shirt. Be alert for the newcomer who is out of his depth, or any chance to smooth out a troubled situation or encourage someone.

Prayer: *Teach us to find Your best blessings when we take the trouble to look after and care for other people, Lord. Lead each member of our family to someone who needs Your love and care today. Amen.*

September 13   HEBREWS 13.1–8

Be satisfied with what you have (v.5, Living Bible).

Comment: Some Mums are always wanting new clothes or the house redecorated. Some Dads think longingly of a new car or a power drill. Some boys are always wanting more track for their railways or a bike with more gears. Some girls covet the latest doll advertised on TV or shoes of the newest style.

Leaning to 'be satisfied' (or contented) with what we have is one of the hardest lessons in life. Paul learned it. He said (Philippians **4.**11) 'I have learned how to get along happily whether I have much or little.'

The secret of contentment is to look at those people who have *less* than you, rather than at those people who have *more*. It makes us all realize how much we have to be thankful for.

Prayer: *Father, thank You for giving us so much. Thank You for our parents, our children, our home, warm clothing, good food and comfortable beds. Thank You for schools and books and TV programmes that enrich our minds, and the beauty of nature to delight our eyes. Give us grateful hearts. Amen.*

September 14   **HEBREWS 13.15–20**

And now may the God of peace ... equip you with all you need for doing his will (v.20, Living Bible).

Comment: Football, riding, skin diving, motor cycling and even gardening all need special equipment. What kind of equipment do you think we need for 'doing his (God's) will ...'?

In Paul's letter to the Ephesians (Ephesians **6.**14–17) he tells us that we need a special 'suit of armour' with a belt of truth, a breastplate of God's approval, shoes to speed us on to tell other people God's good news, a shield of faith, a helmet of salvation, and the sword of God's Holy Spirit (which is the word of God).

Are the members of your family all properly equipped?

Prayer: *Dear Father God, please equip us with all we need for doing Your will, and teach us how to use the sword of Your Spirit, which is the Word of God, to overcome all that is wrong in our lives. For Jesus' sake. Amen.*

September 15   **NEHEMIAH 1.1–6, 11**

When I heard these words I sat down and wept ... and I continued ... praying (v.4, RSV).

Comment: Ask a grandparent, or an elderly relation, what happened in some great disaster or battle when they were younger, and you'll find that they can give you the details straight away; the exact dates too, probably, just as Nehemiah could.

Perhaps one day, we ourselves will look back and say: 'I shall never forget the beginning of that terrible drought in August 1976, when taps had to be turned off; industry was brought to a standstill; cattle and wildlife died, reservoirs dried up and no harvest of vegetables could be gathered in.'

Will history record that we blamed the scientists, or the major powers on the other side of the world? It ought to record how utterly we rely on our Creator God for everything we need—even our very survival. Christian people turned to God for the answer.

Think out: What did Nehemiah insist was the cause of *his* country's misfortunes (v.6b)?

Prayer: *Save us from always blaming circumstances when things go wrong, dear Lord. Help us to recognize that our attitudes and outlook may be wrong and preventing Your good purposes. For Your glory we ask it. Amen.*

September 16   **NEHEMIAH 2.1–8**

'Why is your face sad?' (v.2, RSV).

Comment: It was no good Nehemiah going round singing 'I'm H-A-P-P-Y . . .' when plainly nothing could be further from the truth. No amount of smiler-stickers can change the feelings of a person with a heavy heart. Nehemiah wasn't cheerful company for King Artaxerxes. The king may not have believed in Nehemiah's God, but at least he recognized loyal service when he saw it, and he wanted to do something to help. He felt sorry for Nehemiah.

Never feel that just because somebody isn't committed to Jesus Christ, they are *never* capable of a helpful or considerate good turn. Artaxerxes didn't only allow Nehemiah to go to Jerusalem, he actually made it *easy* for him.

Question: Why do you think things went well for Nehemiah (vs.4 and 8b)?

Prayer: *Heavenly Father, thank You for answering our prayers when we are very unhappy or discouraged, and for showing us that You always have an answer to our problems. Amen.*

September 17   **NEHEMIAH 2.9–16**

So I came to Jerusalem and was there three days. Then I arose in the night . . . (vs.11, 12, RSV).

Comment: It's never easy waiting for something important to happen. Waiting for exam results; waiting for someone you love very much to come home again after a long trip away on his job; waiting for a special day or event which you've been *so* looking forward to. Then, when it comes and the event is delayed, you find you *can* wait a bit longer, because you have learnt to be patient, and because you know it *will* come one day.

Nehemiah had learnt to be patient. He had been given his passport and his visa, and he was allowed to re-enter his beloved country again, under escort, but now he wanted to *make quite sure he knew what ought to be done next*. He didn't want to make any mistakes, so he took his time, and made thorough investigations first, before telling anyone else.

Think spot: If you knew that some friend was considering becoming a missionary what would you advise them to do?

Prayer: *Dear Lord, if You have some special work for us help us to find out carefully what You want us to do. Save us from rushing into plans and decisions which may not be right. For Jesus' sake. Amen.*

September 18   NEHEMIAH 2.17–20

I told them of the hand of my God which had been upon me for good (v.18, RSV).

Comment: After his night amongst the ruins, Nehemiah could have gone to the Jews, priests and nobles and told them that he wanted them to get on with the rebuilding of the walls of Jerusalem, but he didn't do it like that. He began at the beginning, explaining how God had guided him to come to Jerusalem. 'Let *us* build the wall,' he said (v.17). Nehemiah was going to pull his weight although he was the leader. No wonder they all agreed and worked together as a team.

'Let's take some flowers to Auntie Gwen and cheer her up. She's been very depressed lately,' says Mum. 'Do we have to?' groans Terry from the depths of his book. 'Can't we go another day?' asks Sue. 'Take the dog,' suggests Dad. 'He needs the exercise.' It is sometimes very hard to get everyone in a family doing something together as a team, but when we do, it binds us together.

Question: What makes us pull in different directions?

Prayer: *Lord Jesus, show us how to live, work and play together in harmony, for Jesus' sake. Amen.*

September 19   NEHEMIAH 4.1–5

'Will they revive the stones out of the heaps of rubbish . . .?' (v.2, RSV).

Comment: We hear a lot about renovating old houses instead of building new ones these days. Some of the buildings that look old and useless are really very solid and well worth getting into shape again. Nehemiah knew that a good wall could be built out of the old stones even though Sanballat and Tobiah laughed and jeered at what they were doing. Not everything that looks like rubbish is useless.

Nehemiah probably felt like running away or giving up—but what did he do (vs. 4,5)? He knew that it was God's work and so he prayed openly and asked God to help them. We can always look to God for help when we are doing what He wants us to do. **Question:** Should Christians pray the sort of prayer that Nehemiah did? (Look up 1 Peter 2.20–23.)

Prayer: *We pray today for all Christians who are despised or hated because they are trying to please You. Please give them strength and patience. Amen.*

September 20   NEHEMIAH 4.6–14

'The strength of the burden-bearers is failing' (v.10, RSV).
Comment: Richard was helping his father in the garden. Dad mowed the lawns and pruned the trees. Richard gathered up the grass and twigs and carried them to the garden heap. Mum looked out of the window and saw that Richard was tiring and couldn't keep up with Dad. 'Come on,' she said to Nicholas. 'Let's go and help Richard before he wears himself out.'

Building a new wall from nice new stones is easier than re-building one from an old broken-down wall. The rubbish had to be sorted from the good stone and there was so much of it that those who carried the stones were wearing themselves out. There was also another problem. With no wall, and with heaps of rubbish for the enemy to hide behind they were in great danger. Nehemiah saw the problem and arranged the people in such a way that they could defend themselves as they worked.

To think over: God has put us in families so that we can lovingly help and protect one another, especially when we grow weary or are in danger.

Prayer: *We thank You for one another, Lord. Amen.*

September 21   NEHEMIAH 4.15–23

Each with one hand laboured on the work, and with the other held his weapon (v.17, RSV).
Comment: We have 'dual-purpose' buildings and furniture where one thing can be used for two different purposes. Some of us can even *do* two things at the same time. Nehemiah wanted his

132

workers to be able to work and to fight. It was no good being a good builder if you were going to be attacked from behind and your building knocked down. Nor was it much good being a good fighter if the hole in the wall never got mended. Both things had to be done at the same time if they were to win through.

Christians have to be building and fighting at the same time for God's Kingdom. Satan, our enemy, is either looking for a weak spot to undo all our work, or he will try to make us into such aggressive fighters that we never manage to build anything lasting for God.

Question: What two things do we learn about God (vs.15,20)?

Prayer: *Lord God, we pray for all Christian workers today that they may find the right way to build and fight for You, for Your glory. Amen.*

September 22   **NEHEMIAH 5.1–5**

'Other men have our fields and our vineyards' (v 5, RSV).

Comment: You might think that this passage had been written today with all the familiar troubles it describes. First of all they had a problem because there were too many people to feed and not enough corn. That meant spending more money to buy from other countries. Most people had to raise the money by half-selling off their homes, fields and gardens. Others had to borrow from richer folk to pay the taxes to their greedy rulers. Some sold themselves as workers and others sold their children. The rich were getting richer at the expense of the poor who were getting poorer. All these things ring bells in our own world, and, like the Israelites, people are crying out for a solution.

Think spot: We may not be able to do much about the world situation but we can refuse to take advantage of people, and share what we have.

Prayer: *Forgive us for grumbling and complaining, Lord, because we have so much to be thankful for as we look around our world. Help those who are hungry and oppressed. Amen.*

September 23   **NEHEMIAH 5.6–13**

'You are exacting interest, each from his brother' (v.7, RSV).

Comment: 'You mustn't take advantage of him,' a mother said when she caught her two older children cheating their small brother at a game. The little boy was not clever or old enough to realize what they were doing, but he knew that he never seemed to win.

Nehemiah was cross when he saw that the nobles and officials were taking advantage of their fellows by making them sell their lands and even their children as servants in exchange for food. He told them that this was not the way that God wanted them to behave, especially as their enemies were watching all that went on. Whatever would their enemies think of such behaviour from people who were supposed to be children in God's family? It was a good thing that the wrongdoers saw their mistake and were willing to put it right.

Think spot: Our actions almost always affect others for good or for bad. This is especially so in a family.

Prayer: *O Lord, we are sorry for the times when we have taken advantage of someone and let You down. Give us the strength to treat others as we want them to treat us. Amen.*

September 24   **NEHEMIAH 6.1–9**

'Why should the work stop while I leave it and come down to you?' (v.3, RSV).

Comment: The other day we were doing a job and it seemed that the whole world was ganging up to stop us. Two people called and we had to give time to them. The telephone never seemed to stop ringing for more than a few minutes, and eventually we completed what we were doing in the early hours of the morning. I expect you have had days like that, and if you are like us, there are jobs around the house that have got interrupted and they are still waiting to be completed.

Nehemiah and his team were getting on well, but they had constant interruptions (vs. 4,5). They knew that Sanballat and Tobiah wanted to stop them from completing the walls, so Nehemiah had to make a decision. The walls were more important than anything else and even though he was threatened, he would not allow the work to stop.

Think spot: Sometimes we have to stop what we are doing to help a needy person. Sometimes we ought to work on and not allow ourselves to be interrupted by less important things. How do we decide which is which?

Prayer: *Grant us wisdom, Lord, to know what we ought to be doing. Amen.*

'Should such a man as I flee?' (v.11, RSV).
Comment: Imagine that you are supposed to be at the bus stop
to catch a certain bus because you are going on an excursion.
But you are late because you helped the teacher to clear up and
now you are going to miss the bus. Someone suggests you pinch
a bike and leave it at the bus stop—well—just borrow it really.
You know that that would be wrong, so you race back to the
teacher and tell him your trouble. The result is that he gives you
a lift all the way.
    Like Nehemiah, we must not let panic push us into acting
stupidly so that we can later be accused of doing wrong. That
kind of thing could be held against us for a very long time.
Keynote: All things work together for good, to them that love
God (Romans 8.28).
Prayer: *Dear Lord, we know that we are in danger of letting You
down in moments of panic. Help us to turn to You and trust You
to see us through in our difficulties, especially when they crop up
suddenly. Amen.*

The ears of all the people were attentive to the book of the law
(v.3, RSV).
Comment: Newspapermen, politicians, statesmen, scientists and
all sorts of other folk love to compete to tell us what they think
are the most important things we ought to be doing or believing.
But today's reading tells us exactly what the people of Jerusalem
knew to be the most important thing to learn about—GOD'S
WORDS. They were eager to know what God was thinking
about everything; what God was saying about everyone; what
He wanted to say *to* them and what He wanted them to learn.
Nothing else could ever be as important as that.
To think about: How much time do we spend watching TV;
listening to records or the radio; reading books and comics and
talking with our friends? How does this compare with the time
we give to reading God's Word? Perhaps we ought to think
about changing our ways.
Prayer: *Thank You for Your Word, Lord God. Give us the help
of Your Holy Spirit as we read it so that we shall be able to
understand what You are saying to us through it. Amen.*

'This day is holy to the Lord your God; do not mourn or weep'
(v.9, RSV).

Comment: Do you enjoy a holiday? Look very carefully at that
word because it comes from the words 'holy day', which meant
something like Christmas Day and your birthday all rolled into
one. Everyone stopped work and enjoyed a feast together, and
they especially spent time worshipping and thinking about God.
After they had heard God's Word read to them they realized
how far from God they had strayed, but Nehemiah wanted them
to be glad about God's goodness to them and share it with others
(v.10).

Think spot: This is the time of year when churches and schools
hold harvest festivals. We can thank God for His goodness to
us and share what we have with others.

Prayer: *Thank You, Lord, for the wheat and vegetables this year.*
Thank You for water to drink. Thank You for Your Word.
Teach us to share all the good things You give to us, for Your
name's sake. Amen.

And all the assembly ... dwelt in booths (v.17, RSV).

Comment: Does granny ever remind you how bad things were
in the war? Does she tell you how difficult it was to get certain
foods and warm clothing and how most people couldn't drive a
car or eat a banana? Those who had to endure such things were
glad when it was all over, but sometimes it helps us to appreciate
things that we have got when we look back and remember hard
times.

Nehemiah and Ezra wanted a day to 'remember' too. The
Feast of Booths was what they probably called it. Every Israelite
would give thanks for the days when God had protected them
when they had had to live in tents and shelters, called booths,
during their wanderings. They would thank Him too for being
able to live in houses again.

Think spot: Notice that the reading of God's Word was a daily
habit during the feast (v.18). The more we read God's Word,
the more thankful we shall become.

Prayer: *Dear Father, thank You for providing for us day by day and*
for bringing us through our hard times. Amen.

Daniel lived when the Jews were still in Babylon. His experiences show us how God can look after His people in the most difficult circumstances.

September 29   DANIEL 1.1–7

Then the king commanded Ashpenaz, his chief eunuch, to bring some of the people of Israel, both of the royal family and of the nobility (v.3, RSV).
Comment: We have to look back a little to discover why God's people were being taken captive to Babylon. If you have time, read Isaiah 39 and you will see that God had warned the king of Judah what would happen if the king carried on as he had been doing, but Hezekiah refused to take any notice of the warning (Isaiah 39.8). In the book of Daniel we learn that God meant every word of that warning. God does not say one thing and do another, nor does He forget what He has said. It is often our own wilfulness which lands us in trouble. Have you ever been warned about some danger, and you have taken no notice and had to learn the lesson the hard way? How much better if we had listened in the first place!
Question: Do you think 1 Corinthians 10.12 would be a good text to learn by heart today?
Prayer: *Lord, forgive us for thinking that we know best. Help us to take notice of what You say to us in Your Word. Amen.*

September 30   DANIEL 1.8–16

But Daniel resolved that he would not defile himself . . . (v.8, RSV).
Comment: Have you heard sayings like, 'to run with the hare and hunt with the hounds', or, 'to have a foot in both camps'? When we use expressions like these about people we mean that they can change their behaviour to suit the kind of people they are with. Daniel and his friends could have been like that but they had what many of us lack—great determination to be absolutely true to God. The Christian life is not a matter of drifting along doing anything that happens to take our fancy wherever we happen to be. It is a life of discipline and resolve. Satan's aim is to attract us away from God by tempting us with seemingly harmless things—like the king's rich food. We must resolve, resist and determine not to let Satan get even the tiniest hold on our lives, because when he does the result is always defilement—or dirtying.
Thought: A pound of determination is worth a ton of regret.

137

Prayer: *Give us Your strength, dear Lord God, to stand firm for You whatever temptations we face. Amen.*

October 1   DANIEL 1.17-21

As for these four youths, God gave them learning and skill in all letters and wisdom . . . (v.17, RSV).

Comment: When I was a little girl I can remember singing a hymn in Sunday school which started, 'Dare to be a Daniel; dare to stand alone . . .', and then it went on to show that God always cares for those who put their trust in Him. These four young men might easily have become discouraged and refused to learn the Chaldean language and customs. After all, why should they? Their own lives and education had been rudely interrupted and it couldn't have been pleasant to know that they were captives, however well they were being treated. But there were no 'sit-ins' and protest marches from Daniel and his friends. They were prepared to trust God for the outcome, and so they made the best of it all. So well did they do, that they ended up ten times better than anyone else. It was God who gave them the ability (v.17).

Question: Do we believe that God will honour those who honour Him? (See 1 Samuel 2.30.)

Prayer: *O God, give us the courage to be like Daniel and trust You to work things out for us. Amen.*

October 2   DANIEL 2.1-11

'There is not a man on earth who can meet the king's demand . . .' (v.10, RSV).

Comment: The magicians spoke the truth there, no matter what lies they had thought up to gain time. Satan loves to get Christians into this kind of situation where they cannot see a way out, and all around promises disaster. 'Nobody on earth can help me out of this trouble,' we say. And it often comes about because we allow small sinful things to go unchecked. Bit by bit, Satan ties us up in knots. Take this matter of lying, for instance. Brenda was a Christian girl but she allowed herself to tell a lie at school to gain time and get herself out of a scrape. She had to tell another lie to back it up and then she had to keep remembering what she had said so as not to give herself away. She didn't know which way to turn for help, but then she remembered Jesus Christ, and with His strength and help she

138

confessed the whole matter and was forgiven by God and her teacher.

To think over: Hebrews **12.25**.

Prayer: *O God in heaven, we know that no one on earth can help us in our difficulties like You. We thank You for sending Jesus to save us from our sins. Amen.*

October 3 DANIEL 2.12–16

Then Daniel replied with prudence and discretion . . . (v.14, RSV).
Comment: Daniel and his friends were in a tight spot now, all right. They would be killed along with all the wise men because the king had commanded it in a raging temper. See how unreasonable the king was. He said what he would do if the wise men lied to him, and yet when they told the truth, he demanded their death (vs. 8, 12). The king was a very spoilt and selfish man who used his powerful position to get his own way. We sometimes come across people like that who love to throw their weight around, as we say. Daniel was different. He had every reason to be angry, because he hadn't done anything to deserve to die, but he was particularly careful with his words, so that the situation would not become worse than it already was. His wisdom saved the day for himself and his three friends.

To think over: Those who are wise do not let their tempers boil over, because they know that it will only get them into hot water.

Prayer: *Heavenly Father, help us to think first before we speak, especially when we are feeling angry. Keep us from pushing other people around. Amen.*

October 4 DANIEL 2.17–23

'He changes times and seasons; he removes kings and sets up kings . . .' (v.21, RSV).
Comment: As kings go, Nebuchadnezzar was extremely powerful. We have seen in recent readings something of the way in which he made people realize this. But Daniel knew that there was an *all-powerful* King in heaven who could remove Nebuchadnezzar and set up another man in his place whenever He chose. We tend to forget that our God is in charge of the whole universe. We tremble before powerful people on earth, thinking that they can change the whole course of our lives if they wish to do so. Children may feel like this about a headmaster or teacher, and adults about their boss. It is good to remember that nothing can ever happen to us unless God permits it. He has power over

the 'times and seasons', so who on earth is going to tell God
what to do?

Thinking point: 'I have lived a long time and the longer I live
the more convincing proofs I see that God governs in the affairs
of men,' said Benjamin Franklin.

Prayer: *Almighty God, we praise You for Your power over all
things, including our lives. We believe that You allow only those
things to happen to us which are for our good. Amen.*

October 5   DANIEL 2.24–35

'. . . not because of any wisdom that I have . . .' (v.30, RSV).

Comment: Just recently I have heard of a family in which there
are several children all of whom know many things that usually
take the rest of us much longer to learn—if we ever manage to
learn them at all. Then I read of a little boy who could read
about two years before he was old enough for school, and by the
time he went to school he was already doing long-division sums
and had an almost unbeaten record playing chess with grown-
ups. Parents of such children may be tempted to be proud of
themselves for having given life to such brilliance, and the
children themselves may feel that they are a cut above other
children of their age. But pride is not confined to such people.
We all enjoy giving ourselves a pat on the back when we've solved
some problem or won some game.

Question: What lesson can we learn from Daniel about this?

Prayer: *We thank You, O Lord, for the abilities that You have
given to us. We give the glory to You. Amen.*

October 6   DANIEL 2.36–45

'And in the days of those kings the God of heaven will set up a
kingdom which shall never be destroyed, nor shall its sovereignty
be left to another people' (v.44, RSV).

Comment: In today's reading, Daniel shows how the kingdom
which Nebuchadnezzar thinks is all-powerful will eventually
break up. Nebuchadnezzar, the Babylonian king, is like the gold
head of the image of his dream; but the next conqueror (probably from Persia) will be less powerful, like the chest and arms of
silver. After that, a king (probably from Greece) will reign, but
he will be like the bronze parts, and finally a ruler (probably
Roman) will come, whose kingdom will be like a mixture of iron
and clay—strong and weak—that cannot hang together. We
now know that it was during the Roman rule that God set up

His own Kingdom by sending Jesus into the world. Daniel reminds us that God's kingdom will *never* be destroyed.

Thought: However much we fear the breaking up of earthly kingdoms, if we are members of God's Kingdom we are in safe hands for ever.

Prayer: *We are thankful, Lord, that You really are almighty and that Your Kingdom is everlasting. May these truths keep us calm whenever great dangers threaten us. Amen.*

October 7   DANIEL 2.46–49

'Truly, your God is God of gods and Lord of kings, and a revealer of mysteries . . .' (v.47, RSV).

Comment: If we take any notice of the way Nebuchadnezzar talks we see that at last Daniel has convinced him that the God of heaven is the only true God. But like many of us, Nebuchadnezzar did not always live in the same way that he talked. Here he says that he knows God is supreme, and yet we find him continuing to make idols and worshipping the God of heaven along with all these other gods. In other words, the king was giving God only a *share* of his worship when he ought to have been giving God the whole of it. His heart was divided. We are all in danger of saying things with our lips, but living as if our words are not true.

Question: What does God say about being loyal to Him? (See Exodus 20.2–6.)

Prayer: *Help us, dear Lord, to deal with anything that is hindering our worship of You and to love You wholeheartedly. Amen.*

October 8   DANIEL 3.1–7

'You are to fall down and worship the golden image . . . ' (v.5, RSV).

Comment: 'You can take a horse to water but you can't make him drink.' He's got to be thirsty and wanting to drink. His master may talk to him, command him, drag him right into the stream and even beat him with a stick, but if the horse doesn't want to drink, he won't do it. Much the same thing was happening here. The king *commanded* the people to bow down and worship the golden image; he threatened them with a horrible death in the burning fiery furnace if they didn't do it—which was enough in itself to take their minds off any kind of worship. But the people made a show of doing what the king said out of fear. Jesus said that those who worship Him should worship in spirit and in truth—their hearts must be right with God and then their devotion will be real.

Question: Do we make a show of worshipping God by going to church, Sunday school, prayer meetings and Bible study, or do we worship Him truly and go because we really want to please Him?

Prayer: *O Father in heaven, we worship You from our hearts, and we truly want to glorify Your name. Amen.*

October 9   **DANIEL 3.8–18**

'Our God whom we serve is able to deliver us . . . But if not, be it known to you, O king, that we will not serve your gods or worship the golden image which you have set up' (vs.17,18, RSV).

Comment: Daniel's friends faced the king in all his fury and told him that they would not betray their God. They didn't know what would happen. After all, God has never promised that His servants shall escape all suffering in this life. But He guarantees that the life in heaven will more than make up for all that we go through for Him on earth. It must have been a tense moment for them when they heard the king command that the furnace be heated hotter than ever, but they didn't waver. They were like Job, who, when he was in great trouble said, 'Though he (God) slay me, yet will I trust in him' (Job 13.15, AV).

Keynote: Psalm 37.5—'Commit your way to the Lord; trust in him, and he will act.'

Prayer: *Lord Jesus, You did not run away when You were faced with the cross, and You were not spared its pain. Help us to be brave and strong for You. Amen.*

October 10   **DANIEL 3.19–25**

'I see four men loose, walking in the midst of the fire, and they are not hurt; and the appearance of the fourth is like a son of the gods' (v.25, RSV).

Comment: This morning I had to go to the dentist. Two or three others were there and one lady looked as though she would like to run out of the door before she was called! Some of us fear such visits because we don't like the thought of being hurt. What a nice surprise it always seems to be when we get out of the dentist's chair and find that we haven't felt a thing! A little more trust in the dentist would have saved us a lot of anxiety. Daniel's friends must have been afraid of that furnace, but they trusted God and, of course, there He was *with* them in their trouble. The

142

king had tied them up but God set them free in more ways than one. The furnace didn't hurt them, though they had to go through the experience.

To think over: God does not always take us *out* of troubles but He always sees us *through* them.

Prayer: *Be our Companion in all our trials, Lord Jesus, for You give courage and freedom to those who trust in You. Amen.*

October 11   **DANIEL 3.26–30**

'. . . for there is no other god who is able to deliver in this way' (v.29, RSV).

Comment: Are you getting rather impatient with Nebuchadnezzar? He seems to need a lot of convincing, doesn't he? If we look back we see that the king has been at this point before (2.47), but he still will not let go of those idols. Again he shows that he thinks Daniel's God is one of many gods—Oh, yes, undoubtedly God is great, but the king will not commit himself to serve God alone. The best he is willing to do is to stop anyone saying anything against Him. Isn't it amazing that some people can trust God quickly and completely, while others go on year after year and never seem to come to the point where they are willing to give Him complete allegiance and loyalty? They wouldn't say a word against God—but that's as far as they are willing to go.

Question: Can we see ourselves in Nebuchadnezzar?

Prayer: *Almighty God, You have shown in so many ways that You are the only true God. We give ourselves to You completely. Forgive us that we have resisted You for so long. Amen.*

October 12   **DANIEL 5.1–9**

Then the king's colour changed, and his thoughts alarmed him (v.6, RSV).

Comment: How quickly our moods change! Mary jumps happily out of bed on her birthday morning, then hurts her toe against the bedroom door and cries bitterly. John feels very hopeful about his exam results, until he opens the envelope! Breakfast is a happy, cheerful meal until Peter grabs the milk and knocks it over, then Dad is cross and everyone is upset.

King Belshazzar and his drunken friends were noisily drinking their wine from the gold and silver cups belonging to God's holy Temple, and then everyone fell silent as they saw the fingers of a hand writing on the Palace wall. No wonder the king's knees knocked together and the blood drained away from his face.

Because God's warnings are written in His book, and not on our walls, we don't take so much notice of them. But we should. **Warning for us:** John 3.36.

Prayer: *Grant us, O Lord, the good sense to take notice of the warnings that You have given to us in Your Holy Word, and not to take them lightly. Amen.*

October 13   **DANIEL 5.10–16**

'I have heard that you can give interpretations and solve problems' (v.16, RSV).

Comment: What kind of a reputation have we got? It may be good because we are kind and helpful, or bad because we are rude and spiteful. The trouble is that once we get a reputation it usually sticks. There is no doubt that Daniel's reputation was good. For many years, through the reign of Nebuchadnezzar and now in the reign of Belshazzar, Daniel had built up a reputation for living close to God. The queen knew all about him. We shall see in the next chapter how jealous men tried to spoil Daniel's good name without success. True character always wins through in the end. Do you remember that some wicked men tried to spoil Jesus' reputation? They called Him a 'friend of sinners', thinking it would put people off Him, but they were saying only what was true without realizing it, and it did Jesus no harm.

Thought: Our ideal is what we wish we were; our reputation is what other people say we are, but our character is what we really are.

Prayer: *We pray, O Lord, that You will make us to be what You want us to be every moment of every day. Amen.*

October 14   **DANIEL 5.17–23**

'You . . . have not humbled your heart, though you knew all this' (v.22, RSV).

Comment: 'I'm very sorry,' pleaded Mr Parker as the angry farmer accused him of trespassing. 'I didn't realize that it was private property.' Strictly speaking, for Mr Parker or any one of us, ignorance of the law is no excuse: if you don't know what two yellow lines along the side of the road mean, the traffic warden will not let you off for parking on them. 'You should read the Highway Code,' the warden will say to you. King Belshazzar could not say that he didn't know that his life was wicked and selfish. Daniel only spoke the truth when he reminded the king of his father's pride, as well as his own. God had given both kings chances to change their ways but neither had humbled himself before God.

Think spot: The Bible tells us that although sins committed in ignorance will be punished, those people who sin deliberately will be punished much more severely (Luke 12.47, 48).

Prayer: *Almighty God, we have to confess that we have often sinned wilfully, knowing that we were doing wrong. Be merciful to us and help us to turn away from evil, for Christ's sake. Amen.*

October 15   **DANIEL 5.24-31**

'You have been weighed in the balances and found wanting' (v.27, RSV).

Comment: John licked the last two stamps and stuck them on the letters as he helped his mother to catch the post which would be collected in a few minutes. 'Just a minute,' John said, and rushed into the kitchen to pop one of the letters on the scales. 'Mum, this one is overweight. Bring another stamp, or Grandpa won't be too pleased when he has to pay double at the other end.' That letter had been 'weighed in the balances and found wanting'. An extra stamp was needed to meet the requirements of the Post Office. When we come to Belshazzar, it was his life that hadn't measured up to God's requirements and an extra stamp couldn't put *that* right! God's standard is perfection (Matthew 5.48), which means that we are *all* 'found wanting'. It is a good thing for us that when Jesus died on the cross He paid all that was due, so that we who trust in Him can safely reach our destination.

Thought: 'All have sinned and fall short of the glory of God' (Romans 3.23).

Prayer: *We have failed, like Belshazzar, Lord, but we thank You for paying our penalty. Amen.*

October 16   **DANIEL 6.1-9**

Then the presidents and the satraps sought to find a ground for complaint against Daniel with regard to the kingdom; but they could find no ground for complaint or any fault, because he was faithful, and no error or fault was found in him (v.4, RSV).

Comment: 'CLERGYMAN TAKES CONTINENTAL HOLI-DAY ON CHURCH FUNDS.' That headline sold a good many extra copies! 'Fancy,' people said, 'who would have thought a Christian would do a thing like that?' You can be sure the newspaper editors would not have given it such a prominent place if the deed had been done by an ordinary clerk in an insurance office. At school or at work, particularly if we have a high position, we should be the best that we can be for God *all the time*, like Daniel, because as soon as anyone can find fault with our work, we are letting our Master down. We can write across Daniel's life, 'No complaints'.

Question: What do people write across our lives?

Prayer: *O Lord, the Bible says that You are able to keep us from falling and to present us faultless before God. We want You to do this for us, for Your name's sake. Amen.*

October 17   DANIEL 6.10–18

He got down upon his knees three times a day and prayed and gave thanks before his God, as he had done previously (v.10, RSV).
Comment: I heard of a man who wrote his wife a love letter *every day* of his life, though he lived with her! To him it was a matter of the highest importance. My father-in-law developed diabetes towards the end of his life and *every day* he had to inject himself with insulin: it was a matter of life and death. We all do things every day because they are important, like cleaning our teeth, but I wonder if we include prayer in our list. To some Christians, prayer is a thing they do because it provides a vital life-line to God. To others it is a dreary performance to be endured, while still others hardly ever think about it. There's no doubt about the importance that Daniel gave to it, even though he was risking his life every time he prayed.

Questions: How much importance do we give to prayer? Did Jesus give it high priority? (Mark 1.35.)

Prayer: *O God, may our love for You be so great that we shall want to talk to You. Amen.*

October 18   DANIEL 6.19–24

. . . those men who had accused Daniel were brought and cast into the den of lions (v.24, RSV).
Comment: King Darius had spent a sleepless night. He realized that through his own selfish decrees he had been trapped into doing something that he didn't want to do—and that must have made him full of anger and sorrow. But the wicked men who had forced Darius to have Daniel thrown to the lions soon found that they too had trapped themselves. Daniel was brought out of the den unharmed but they were thrown in and perished. In

other words, they got a taste of their own medicine. Like Daniel, David too had seen this kind of thing happen to his enemies. When he had been running from King Saul he was able to write, 'They dug a pit in my way, but they have fallen into it themselves' (Psalm 57.6). Both Daniel and David remained safe because they trusted in the same God.

Thought: The apostle Paul put it this way: 'He who sows to his own flesh will from the flesh reap corruption; but he who sows to the Spirit will from the Spirit reap eternal life' (Galatians 6.8). What does this mean?

Prayer: *Deliver us, O God, from wicked men. We trust in You. Amen.*

October 19   DANIEL 6.25–28

I make a decree, that in all my royal dominion men tremble and fear before the God of Daniel (v.26, RSV).

Comment: What a change in king Darius! And how different was the decree he made *this* time, compared with his earlier decree of verse 7! Daniel and his God were to come first from now on; and even though we may decide that Darius was horribly cruel to throw Daniel's jealous enemies to the lions, at least it was his way of showing whose side he was on! Darius was certainly convinced, even if he were not converted.

There are many people whose lives have been completely changed, and given back to God, when they have seen for themselves how miraculously God has saved another person's life. It may be that God has healed that person, or saved him in some incredible way from tragedy; and the amazement and relief for the unbeliever has resulted in his conversion and faith in Jesus Christ. Don't just be impressed when you see God's power for someone else. Accept His power for your own life.

Question: Darius' actions in these verses suggest two specific things we should do when we first give our lives to Jesus Christ. What are they?

Prayer: *Turn verses 26 and 27 into a prayer of praise in your own words.*

October 20   1 JOHN 1.5–10

If we say we have fellowship with him while we walk in darkness, we lie . . . (v.6, RSV).

Comment: I wonder whether you have seen advertisements for jewellery stones which, the adverts claim, are so like diamonds

147

that even experts cannot tell the difference? Sadly, there are Christians who are rather like those stones! They *say* things that Christians would say; even *do* things that Christians would do—things like going to church, praying or reading the Bible. But somehow their attitudes, lifestyle, seems not to ring true to the teachings of Jesus.

God certainly doesn't want us to go through life judging other people—but He does want us to be genuinely His children ourselves. By our faith in Jesus Christ as Saviour, God receives us as His children; but then, very reasonably because He loves us, He says, 'live like My children. With My Son as your example and My Spirit as your Guide.

Prayer: *Lord, we want to be real in Your eyes. Help us. Amen.*

October 21   **1 JOHN 2.1–6**

By this we may be sure that we know him, if we keep his commandments (v.3, RSV).

Comment: Can you be *sure* the bus you catch on Monday will take you to work or school? It always has. So that you believe it will again. And so you hop aboard. That's *faith*—and you can't live without it.

People sometimes say, 'How can I know that God is to be trusted? That if I ask Jesus to come into my life, He will really do so? And what difference will it make?'

Big questions! To which John gives at least *one* answer here. 'We may be sure that we know him' when we find ourselves able to keep His laws, which previously we found a problem. Perhaps we have found it hard to love people . . . or have tended to gossip . . . or have a bad temper. Now we trust the Lord Jesus—and find that God is helping us keep our problem under control.

To think about: What has God done in the life of your family recently which helps you to believe in Him?

Prayer: *Thank You, Lord, for making us able to do things we couldn't do in our own strength. Help us to live for You today. Amen.*

October 22   **1 JOHN 2.7–11**

Beloved, I am writing you no new commandment . . . Yet I am writing you a new commandment (vs.7,8, RSV).

Comment: How very odd! People sometimes say the Bible is full of contradictions—and here it really looks as though John is saying different things in these two verses. But is he?

● 'NO new commandment'. God's commandment that we should love one another is *certainly* not new—see Matthew 22.37-39.

● 'A new commandment', or rather, a new experience of the old commandment, comes when God Himself helps us to be loving to others. And not only to the ones we instinctively like.

Our 'brother' or our 'neighbour' may be a dreadful person but we should not hate them however bad they are. We must try to see that it is possible to hate the things people do without hating the people who do them. Parents often hate the things their children do, but they go on loving their children. Jesus hates the sinful things we do, but He never fails to love us.

Question: Do you think we can learn to hate sin and love people like that?

Prayer: *Help us to learn this hard lesson, Lord, for Your sake. Amen.*

October 23   1 JOHN 2.12–17

Do not love the world or the things in the world (v.15, RSV).

Comment: 'Have you heard the one about . . . ?' 'It can't hurt just to have a look . . .' 'What's wrong with wanting a harmless party? You never let us have any fun . . .'

It isn't that the apostle John was a kill-joy. Far from it. He knew all about the excitement and adventure of following Jesus of Nazareth; he knew the thrill and joy of his new life in Christ. He knew, too, something of the cost of following Jesus. So he doesn't mince words when it comes to warning others who want to follow Jesus.

Satan is crafty. He doesn't always come rushing in with an 'obvious' temptation to sin; he presents an attractive sample. 'Try this—a little can't hurt . . .' John tells us to be on our guard. When in doubt, it's best to ask, 'Will this really help me to live for God?' It's not how near one can get to sin that matters, but how close one can come to God.

Thought: Satan only needs a foothold.

Prayer: *Lord God, help us to recognize Satan when he tries to draw us away from following You. Amen.*

October 24   1 JOHN 3.11–18

Let us not love in word or speech but in deed and in truth (v.18, RSV).

Comment: If a mother kept on saying that she loved her baby

149

without seeing that the baby was clean, clothed and fed, we should think it a funny kind of love. If a young man told a girl he loved her, but never bothered to see her or write to her, she would soon wonder what kind of love he had for her. Real love is always followed by some kind of action and it always costs us something. When we truly love someone, we give ourselves to them. We don't mind what we do for them. We want the best for them.

God not only *told* us that He loved us, but *He sent Jesus* to die for us (v.16). We couldn't have more action at greater cost than that. When God's great love for us sinks in, and we love Him in return, it will show in the way we serve Him and love others for His sake.

To think about: In what ways can we show the other members of our family that we love them? How about our neighbours and those in our church?

Prayer: *Lord God, thank You for Your great love in sending Jesus for us. May our love for You show in the way we live for You. Amen.*

October 25   1 JOHN 3.19–24

'God is greater than our hearts' (v.20, RSV).
Comment: The boy with the suspicious-looking bulge to his coat pockets was 'laying down the law' to his eager friends. 'Of *course* it's all right to pinch sweets from shops. Big shops anyway. They can afford it. And if they don't want us to, they jolly well ought to look after their stock better!'

Do you think he was right? Of course you don't! But maybe there are other things that *we* think are 'all right'—but which God's Word says are all wrong! Being jealous, for instance. Or spreading gossip. Or the way we behave toward parents whom God's law says we should 'honour'. It is easy to say, 'I don't see that it matters'—and go on in our own way. Maybe it sounds odd, making 'love' a matter of commandment (23); but if God has told us to do the two things that it says in verse 23—who are we to think differently?

Prayer: *We want to keep right with You, Lord. Forgive us for all our wrongdoing and give us Your Holy Spirit to help us to obey You. Amen.*

In this is love, not that we loved God, but that he loved us and sent his Son (v.10, RSV).
Comment: Do you think that it's too early to start thinking about Christmas presents? I know at least one shop near my home that has Christmas cards on sale in August. But today's reading reminds us of the wonderful Christmas present God gave us, when Jesus was born. Do you see what that present is? 'LIFE,' says John. 'God sent his only Son into the world, that we might *live* through him.' *Really live*—as opposed to merely existing, without the happiness of knowing how much God loves us.

Of course, knowing that God loves *us* must make a difference to the way we treat *other people*—see verse 11. Does it?
Question: Is there someone to whom we are by habit unkind . . . unloving . . . impatient?
Prayer: *May Your love grow in us, dear Lord, so that we can love others as You have asked us to do. Amen.*

There is no fear in love (v.18, RSV).
Comment: What kinds of things are you afraid of? It might be the dark; thunder and lightning; hospital; war. Perhaps you are even afraid of God. 'Fear has to do with punishment,' says verse 18. We are afraid of things when we think they are going to harm us, and in a way we are really being afraid of God because we are not sure what He is going to do to us.

God does not want us to think of Him as some great ogre just waiting to pounce on us. He wants us to belong to Him in a loving relationship, trusting Him completely (v.16). Then when we meet Him we shall not dread it, but look forward to it with confidence.
Think spot: The next time something makes us afraid, let us try to remember that we are with God and He is with us. It will make a difference.
Prayer: *Thank You, Lord God, for promising to be with us always. May Your love for us and ours for You keep us from being afraid. Amen.*

And his commandments are not burdensome (v.3, RSV).

Comment: 'Just look at Eric', cries Sue. 'He's tidying up the books for the new Geography teacher. He wouldn't have done that for the old one.' The way we feel about someone often affects what we are willing to do for them.

In our families, our feelings show for one another in the way we behave. We either help willingly because we love one another, or we moan because it's our turn again to do some duty and we try to get out of it.

God says that we can tell the true members of His family by the way they love one another and want to help in any way they can. They don't find obeying God's commands a burden, but a joy (vs. 2–4).

Question: How do we feel about worshipping God, praying and reading the Bible? Is it all a burden or something we enjoy?

Prayer: *Forgive us for the times when we have been selfish and unloving in our family, Lord. Teach us how to enjoy serving You. Amen.*

God gave us eternal life, and this life is in his Son (v.11, RSV).

Comment: Imagine being very ill and the doctor saying to you, 'Here are several bottles of medicine. This one tastes nice; this one is a pretty colour; this one has some very expensive drugs in it, but this is the one that will make you better'. You would be sensible enough to take the last one, wouldn't you, because that would mean life to you.

God says that the only people who will have eternal life are those who take His Son to be their personal Saviour. 'He who has the Son has life; he who has not the Son has not life' (v.12). It's as simple as that. How good of God to tell us how we can have eternal life so that we know when we have got it (v.13).

Question: In what other ways do some people think they can obtain eternal life (e.g. going to church)?

Prayer: *You have told us simply and clearly how we can be sure that we have eternal life, Heavenly Father. Give us the courage to make sure that we have it. Amen.*

'Little children, keep yourselves from idols' (v.21, RSV).
Comment: I know a family who didn't agree about *many* things.
In fact they seemed to disagree about almost everything. But one
thing they *did* agree about, was that the Bible was 'all rubbish'.
'All that about people choosing between God and idols!' they
snorted; 'surely that can't apply to people today?' And then they
went on to explain how each one of the family had 'commitments'
which made it impossible for them to worship God in church on
Sunday. A car to wash . . . a football match to play . . . a pony to
groom . . . a stamp collection to attend to.

Of course, in our hearts most of us who are Christians *know*
when we are merely making excuses for not giving to God our
love, worship and service. Verse 20 explains *why* we know. But
still we can make our excuses, forgetting how things good in
themselves can become our idols, when we put them before God.
Prayer: *Lord, in all things, help us to put You first. Amen.*

---

*Ezra and Nehemiah have told us about the people returning to
Judah. Many years earlier Isaiah had prophesied that this would
happen. The chapters we shall read over the next two weeks describe
how God was going to help His people. Look out especially for signs
of God's power and love and the joy of His people. Look out, too,
for prophecies that go beyond what God would do when He brought
the people back from Babylon to what He did for us in Jesus Christ.*

October 31   ISAIAH 40.1–5

'Make straight in the desert a highway for our God' (v.3, RSV).
Comment: Highways in the desert; valleys filled up; mountains
levelled; uneven ground flattened and rough places smoothed out
are all ways of saying that things are different when God begins
to work. God can deal with all kinds of difficulties.

The Israelites had been punished in Babylon and now God was
going to help them to go back to their own land and start again.
They needed encouraging to believe what God said and act upon
it.

If you have been sent to bed for disobedience, you know what it
feels like when Mum calls to say that you can join the family
again. You still feel put out by what has happened and you need
courage to go back and face them all. But when they welcome you
and encourage you to join in what they are doing, you know that
all is forgiven and you make a fresh start.

To think over: God encourages us to trust in Jesus and promises that life will be different if we do—like walking on a highway instead of a desert.

Prayer: *Thank You, Lord, for all Your precious promises. Teach us how to trust You day by day and may our lives show others the way to follow You. Amen.*

November 1   ISAIAH 40.6–11

He will feed his flock like a shepherd (v.11, RSV).

Comment: We all spend a great deal of our lives making sure that we have somewhere to live, enough to wear and to eat and money saved up in case of need, but none of us knows how long we shall be able to benefit from these things. They make us feel secure but we have to agree that verse 7 is right.

Sheep don't worry about any of these things. The shepherd plans where they will sleep, and he leads them to the places where they will find grass to eat. The shepherd gives special help to the little lambs and to any sheep needing extra care (v.11).

God wants us to trust Him like sheep trust their shepherd. Of course, this does not mean that we must all give up our jobs and stop living in houses; buying food to eat or wearing clothes; saving money and making plans for the future. It means that we should not rely on these things so much that we do not put our trust in God.

To think about: Read Luke 12.16–21

Prayer: *Thank You, Lord God, for all the good things of life, but thank You most of all for Your loving care which lasts for ever. Amen.*

November 2   ISAIAH 40.12–17

All the nations are as nothing before him (v.17, RSV).

Comment: Have you read the story of Gulliver in Lilliput? The tiny people looked like minute insects below him so that he could have squashed dozens of them under his big feet.

When we think of great nations like America, Russia and China, it seems to us that they are giants and the smaller nations like insects in the world. It is frightening at times to consider what these giants might do to one another, let alone what they could do to the little nations.

Our reading today helps us to realize that God is in control. To Him great nations are no bigger than a tiny droplet of water splashed from a full bucket, or a speck of dust left on the scales when the flour has been weighed (v.15). The nations may jostle and threaten one another, but they cannot tell God what to do, nor even tell Him what they will do. He made them, though some of them do not believe in Him, and they can do only what God allows.

Question: If nations are as nothing to God, what about me? See Luke 12.7.

Prayer: *You are truly great, Lord God, and we worship You today. Amen.*

November 3   ISAIAH 40.18–24

To whom then will you liken God, or what likeness compare with him? (v.18, RSV).

Comment: When you have had your photograph taken, you wait eagerly for the prints to come. Have you ever been terribly disappointed and said 'That's not at all like me'? You are comparing the photograph with what you see yourself to be like in the mirror, and someone might tease you by saying, 'The camera never lies!', but you are sure that it does.

People who make idols of wood or stone to represent God are making a lie. God cannot be compared with idols that have been made by men and that cannot speak or move.

Most of us don't have wooden idols to help us to think about God but we all have our own idea of what we think God is like. How powerful do we believe Him to be? How gracious and loving? How personal?

Question: Is God likely to be disappointed by my idea of what He is like? Is He greater than my idols, whether they are 'pop' idols or sports idols or anything else?

Prayer: *No one and nothing can compare with You, Lord. May we realize what You are truly like and give You the honour that is due to You. Amen.*

November 4   ISAIAH 40.25–31

He gives power to the faint (v.29, RSV).

Comment: We all know what it is like to be tired and weary. Baby gets tired of his toys; school children of studying; young people of dashing about; Mum of housework; Dad of his job and perhaps of travelling; Grandpa of pottering in the garden and Granny of knitting. There is always so much to be done and we seem to run out of strength to cope with it. It is wonderful when someone offers to help us when we are weary. We feel much better right away, and sometimes we surprise ourselves by getting through a lot more than we thought possible.

The Lord God never grows tired and weary. In fact, He has enough strength to give some to us when we feel we can't go on. Human helpers grow weary like we do, so their help is limited. God's help is not only sufficient for us but it goes on and on all through our lives. Read verse 31 again.

Question: What do you think 'waiting' for the Lord means?

Prayer: *We need Your strength, Lord. Forgive us when we try to manage without You. Give us all the strength we need for today, for Your name's sake. Amen.*

November 5 ISAIAH 42.1–9

'A light to the nations' (v.6, RSV).

Comment: We have been reading a lot recently about the greatness of God; how He never dies nor grows weary and how He needs no one to tell Him what to do. Perhaps this has made you feel very small and useless and you wonder what part you have to play in the big world which God has made.

Today we see that God has got a job for those who love Him and are His people. He wants us to be like a light in the dark world, showing up the things that are wrong and helping people to see that God's ways are best. When we see people being treated unjustly, we can stand up for the right. Just recently a Russian prisoner has been released because someone cared about him and worked for years to bring about his freedom from the unjust treatment he had been receiving. Small voices can be heard and things can be changed. For Christians, with the Lord on their side, there is no limit to what can be done (vs.6, 7).

Keynote: 'I am the Lord, I have called you' (v.6).

Prayer: *Lord, we are often afraid of standing up for things that are good and right because so many are against us. We rely on Your strength. Amen.*

November 6 ISAIAH 43.1–7

'You are precious in my eyes, and honoured, and I love you' (v.4, RSV).

Comment: If a friend whom we love very much goes off with someone else and doesn't care about us any more, we find it difficult to go on loving them, and we would think very carefully before we took them back as our friend again. Love and trust go hand in hand. When we can't trust someone, it affects our love for them.

What a wonderful God we have, because He goes on loving people when they have let Him down again and again. God's people had disobeyed Him badly and yet today's verses show us that God was willing to take them back as His friends again. Look at some of the words He uses to describe them: 'precious', 'honoured', and 'loved'. He was willing to forgive them and put the wrong things right, even though they didn't deserve it. God has not changed. He 'showed His love for us in that while we were yet sinners Christ died for us' (Romans 5.8).

Think: God says, 'I love you' (v.4).

Prayer: *We are glad that You love us so much, dear Lord. Thank You for making us Your friends in spite of all our failures. Amen.*

November 7   ISAIAH 45.18–25

'Declare and present your case' (v.21, RSV).

Comment: Imagine a courtroom where a case is being tried between two people, one of whom is deaf and dumb. The deaf and dumb person cannot hear a word nor say anything to defend himself. An idol made of wood could do no better (v.20).

Some of the Israelites had started to worship idols instead of God whilst they were captives in Babylon. When God came to rescue them they still clung to their idols. God told them that if they wanted to be saved, they must believe Him when He said, 'I am God, and there is no other' (v.22). They must choose between the true God and their idols.

We, too, can be in grave danger of clinging to things which keep us from trusting in God. They can take up all our time, attention and affection so that God is pushed out.

Question: What are some of the idols that keep us away from God in these days?

Prayer: *Heavenly Father, we believe that You are the one true God and that there is no other. May we give You first place in our lives. Amen.*

November 8   ISAIAH 52.7–10

Good tidings of good (v.7, RSV).

Comment: For a very long time, we have been waiting to put up a prefabricated building at the back of our church, because we need more room. All kinds of things had to be looked into before it could be done and we grew weary of telling people that we hoped to have it soon. We talked to God about it constantly and then, at last, the good news came that the plans had been passed and we could go ahead. We felt like singing the kind of song that Isaiah wrote here.

Not only the enemies of Israel, but also some of God's own people must have doubted that God would bring them back to Jerusalem. Then, one day, it all began to happen. God sent good tidings—or news—to His people that all was well and they were going to be saved.

Question: What 'good tidings of good' has God sent to us through His Son?

Prayer: *We praise You, Lord God, that You still do wonderful things for Your people. Thank You for the greatest good news of all time which You have sent to us through Your Son, our Saviour. Amen.*

November 9   ISAIAH 52.13–15 and 53.1–3

He was despised and rejected by men (53.3, RSV).

Comment: There are a number of places in the Old Testament where the writers have put down things which were not only about their own day, but also had a meaning for the future. This passage is one of them, and a great deal of what we have read in today's verses came true when Jesus came into the world. He was God's Servant sent by God to rescue us, just as God rescued His people from their enemies in Isaiah's day.

Imagine a mum going all the way to school in a storm with her little boy's raincoat so that he could keep dry on the way home. When he came out of school the boy refused to wear it and dashed off in the rain leaving his mum to come back by herself. The boy 'despised'—or 'thought nothing of' what his mother had done, and he 'rejected'—or 'refused to have anything to do with' her or the raincoat.

Think spot: Some people treat Jesus in this way and refuse the salvation which He has died to bring to us.

Prayer: *Lord Jesus, You still offer Your salvation to any who will accept You as Saviour. May we not turn away from You today. Amen.*

November 10   ISAIAH 53.4–9

With his stripes we are healed (v.5, RSV).

Comment: As we saw yesterday, Isaiah was not only writing about events at that time but also about the future when Jesus

158

would come. God promised to send His Servant. Isaiah didn't know when He would come but he wrote down what God told him. We are able to look back on it and see that things happened to Jesus just as Isaiah described them.

Verses 4–6 remind us why Jesus needed to come and save us. The false trial that Jesus went through, refusing to say a word, is mentioned (vs.7, 8; see Matthew 27.12–14). Crucifixion was the way that criminals were put to death and Jesus was hung on a cross between two wicked men (v.9; see Luke 23.32). Then He was buried in a rich man's grave which Joseph of Arimathea had made for himself (v.9; see Luke 23.50–53).

Remember: The next time someone laughs at you for believing the Bible, or asks you how you can be sure that what it says is true, show them Isaiah 53 and the places in the Gospels where the prophecies came true. This may encourage them to trust Jesus too.

Prayer: *Thank You for Your Word, the Bible, Lord God. Strengthen our faith as we read it day by day. Amen.*

He shall see the fruit of the travail of his soul and be satisfied (v.11, RSV).

Comment: If you have a garden you will know what a lot of back-breaking hard work—or travail—has to go into it before you can gather the fruit and enjoy the results of all the hard work. On the other hand, if one seed potato is planted and dies, see how many you can dig up a few months later.

God promised that Jesus would see the results of His work and cruel death for us, which shows that God planned that Jesus would rise from the dead, and now we know it too. Day by day ever since, men and women and boys and girls have been putting their trust in Jesus and giving their lives over to Him. This is the 'fruit' that Jesus is gathering and it makes all that He did for us satisfying and worth while. One day, Jesus will present the 'fruit' that He has gathered to God, His Father in heaven.

Question: Are we among the 'fruit' that Jesus wants to see for all His hard work (Ephesians 5.27)?

Prayer: *Lord, we do not deserve all that You have done for us, but we are glad that You loved us enough to die for us. We want to please You and be among the fruit that You have gathered. Amen.*

'Hear, that your soul may live' (v.3, RSV).

Comment: 'Dinner's ready!' calls Mum, 'Come and get it!' And she puts the roast beef and Yorkshire pudding on the table. Jimmy takes not the slightest notice, but goes on playing with his toys and chewing his gum. No wonder Mum gets impatient. 'Now listen to me,' she says. 'Get rid of that gum and come and eat something that will do you good. If you don't come whilst it's on the table, you will be too late.'

Like Jimmy, the Israelites needed rousing from their stupidity. They had longed to go back to their own land but as the years had gone by they had got used to life in Babylon and lost interest in God. They seemed content with second-best. They were wasting their lives on things in Babylon that could never satisfy them or make them happy. If they didn't get up and follow God's directions now, it might be too late (v.6).

Question: In what ways can we work for that which does not satisfy (v.2)?

Prayer: *Please help us, Lord, always to seek and work for the things that will really satisfy us. Amen.*

'It shall accomplish that which I purpose' (v.11, RSV).

Comment: Have you ever heard old people say, 'He's as good as his word'? It is a saying that comes from the days when men did not write down their agreements, but made promises in words. A man who was 'as good as his word' was one you could rely on to do what he said. In other words, he kept his promises.

God is 'as good as His Word'. He promised the Israelites that He would rescue them and give them a new and satisfying life. They would have joy, peace and prosperity (vs. 12, 13), if they would trust and obey God. They could absolutely rely on this just as they relied on the rain to water their crops and make them grow (v.10).

God is 'as good as His Word' today. He wants to keep His promises. As we read the Bible day by day we can look out for these promises. He had us in mind when He made them, and all we have to do is trust Him.

A promise to claim today: 'You shall go out in joy, and be led forth in peace' (v.12).

Prayer: *Heavenly Father, we thank You for Your promises to us which we know You want to keep if we will only trust and obey You. Help us to do so. Amen.*

A garland instead of ashes (v.3, RSV).
Comment: Perhaps you have heard people jokingly say that they
are in 'sackcloth and ashes' when they are apologizing for something. In Isaiah's day, people used to put on old clothes and sit
in ashes on the floor as a sign that they were very sad and miserable, perhaps about a death in the family or some calamity. Some
of the Israelites had done this when they were taken captive to
Babylon.

Isaiah came along with God's good news that they were going
to be rescued and go back to their own land (v.1). Their misery
would be turned into joy (v.3), and they would want to serve
God again (v.4).

Jesus used the words we have been reading when He began
to preach and teach in Galilee (Luke 4.16-21). He said that these
words were being fulfilled—or were coming true—in Him. Just
as the Israelites were brought out of their captivity in Babylon,
so Jesus came to rescue us from being Satan's captives.
Question: Some people don't want to be rescued. Why do you
think this is?
Prayer: *Thank You for Your good news, Lord. Please help us to be
truly joyful. Amen.*

'But be glad and rejoice for ever in that which I create' (v.18,
RSV).
Comment: There are lots of things which make us sad. Some of
them are listed here. Does it upset you when someone is in
trouble? What do you feel like when you hear of the death of a
baby or a good grown-up when there are so many bad people
left alive? It is very sad to watch a man build a house and then
not be able to live in it, or to see someone work hard in his garden
and not be able to eat and enjoy what he has grown. Life can seem
very unfair and people shake their heads and wonder what will
become of them.

Things will not always be unfair. God is going to do something
about it when He sets up His Kingdom. There will be complete
happiness and peace in His Kingdom—no war, no vandalism,
no cruelty, no robbery, no illness and no death (see Revelation
21.1-4).
Think: Who will be there to enjoy it all? 'My people' says God.
Those who have made God's Son their King. Only God's people
could be happy in a Kingdom like that.

Prayer: *Lord God, we realize how wonderful Your Kingdom will be. Help us to remember this when life seems unfair, for Jesus' sake. Amen.*

Do you perhaps ever think of God as a soft-hearted Father who will make life easy and trouble-free all the time for His children? Your own fathers can't do that, and it wouldn't help us to grow up if they did anyway. God was waiting for Job to find out that God was far greater and more wonderful than any of the unhappy things which happened to Job. It was like a new beginning.

November 16   JOB 1.1–5

'It may be that my sons have sinned' (v.5, RSV).
Comment: Job was a very rich farmer and with all those animals and servants to look after, he was probably a very busy man. But he wasn't too busy to take an interest in his ten children, and because he loved God so much, he wanted his children to live good God-fearing lives too. Job knew that in all the excitement of birthday parties, they might forget themselves and do something silly, so he made it his business to see that wrong things were put right on the spot and not allowed to go on until they became too big to deal with. Job faced facts. He knew that his children were not perfect.

When God created a 'family', He meant it to be a group of people who loved and cared for one another through thick and thin.
To think about: In a family we should be able to share everything, good and bad, without fear of being misunderstood.
Prayer: *Heavenly Father, teach us how to care for one another in our family, even when we have failed in some way, for Jesus' sake. Amen.*

November 17   JOB 1.6–12

'Hast thou not put a hedge about him and his house and all that he has on every side?' (v.10, RSV).
Comment: A good job, a well-built house and a happy family spell success and security for most people. The firm may go through hard times, the house need a few jobs doing on it and the children get measles or mumps from time to time, but we get over these things and all seems plain sailing for the future. Our way of life seems permanent.

But we get a little peep behind the scenes in heaven in our reading today. Satan believed that Job loved God only because everything was going well for him. That sounded reasonable. What would happen if Job lost everything? Would he still trust God? We shall see tomorrow.

Today's lesson: Satan is always active in the world. He is allowed to test people, but God has the last word (v.12).

Question: What should Christians learn from this? (See 1 Peter 5.8.)

Prayer: *Thank You, Lord, for warning us about Satan. Teach us how to watch out for him and strengthen us to resist him. Amen.*

November 18   **JOB 1.13–22**

Now there was a day . . . (v.13, RSV).

Comment: Job got up in the morning in the ordinary way. His eldest son was having a party, and all his brothers and sisters were there. The servants were ploughing and looking after the animals; Job was at home, probably dealing with the business side of running his farm as he had often done before.

Then CRASH! Something happened out of the blue (vs.15, 16). One calamity was followed by another, as often seems to happen (vs.17–19), until Job must have wondered if he was having a horrible nightmare. Everything was gone, and yet not really everything because God was still there. Instead of turning to God and asking what he had done to deserve this treatment, Job fell on his face before God and worshipped the One who has the right to act as He pleases, and who never makes mistakes (vs. 20–22).

Think spot: God always has a purpose in all that happens to us. Job's prayer is a good one to remember in times of trouble (v.21).

Prayer: *We believe that You always do what is best for us in the end, Lord. Give us a firm trust in You. Amen.*

November 19   **JOB 2.1–6**

Satan answered the Lord (v.2, RSV).

Comment: The scene changes again and we find Satan slinking into God's presence. He has failed with Job so far but he will not give up. He has got another idea up his sleeve. 'Try hurting Job physically,' he suggests. 'That will make him turn against You. No man holds out when his own skin is at stake.'

We read that Satan spends his time going 'to and fro on the

earth', and 'walking up and down on it' (**1.7; 2.2**). God has given us lots of warnings about Satan and He tells us that we must be on our guard. Satan is cunning (2 Corinthians **11.3, 14**; the 'serpent' is another name for Satan). Even Jesus did not escape Satan's attack (Matthew **4.3–10**).

Question: How did Jesus cope with Satan (Matthew **4.10, 11**)?

Prayer: *Lord Jesus, You understand what it is like to be attacked by Satan. We are no match for him without Your strength. Thank You for promising to help us to overcome when we put our trust in You. Amen.*

November 20   JOB 2.7–13

In all this Job did not sin with his lips (v.10, RSV).

Comment: Our postman delivered a letter with a Christian sticker on it. 'I used to go to chapel,' he said, 'but I don't go any more.' 'Why is that?' we asked. 'Well,' he replied, 'my mother was a chapel-goer all her life. She worked hard for God—anyone in our village will tell you that.' 'What happened?' we asked. 'She suffered a long and painful illness with cancer,' he explained. 'Hardly anyone from the chapel came to visit her after the first few weeks. If God allowed that after all my mother had done, I can't believe He's a God of love, so I don't go now.'

There were lots of wrong ideas in the postman's mind when he blamed God for not giving his mother special treatment, but there were sad truths too. Job's friends came and sat with him in the ashpit for seven days and nights just keeping him company when he was too ill to talk. The postman's mother's friends, even though they claimed to be Christians, grew weary of visiting when the illness dragged on.

Question: How can people learn the truth about God when some of His children do not behave as they should?

Prayer: *Be close to those who are ill today, dear Lord. Send them loving friends to help them. We do want to show others Your love through the way we behave towards them. Amen.*

November 21   JOB 8.17

'If you are pure and upright, surely then he will rouse himself for you and reward you . . .' (v.6, RSV).

Comment: 'If you will do this, I will do that,' we often say. We make a bargain. 'You can borrow my bike if I can borrow your scooter'; 'I'll give you one of my sweets if you will give me one

164

of yours'; 'You can come with me if you promise to be good,' and so on. The word 'if' is very small but very powerful.

Bildad thought that *if* a person was good, God would reward him. But God does not say that we must be good before He will have anything to do with us. *If* He did, none of us would stand a chance. Thankfully His mercy does not depend on our purity and uprightness (Ephesians 2.8, 9), but on His love. 'God shows His love for us in that while we were yet sinners Christ died for us' (Romans 5.8).

To think over: All God's children have troubles and testings, but God sees them through.

Prayer: *Heavenly Father, Your love is wonderful. May we never doubt it especially when we are in trouble. Amen.*

November 22   JOB 19.7–19

'Those whom I loved have turned against me' (v. 19, RSV).

Comment: When a person has done something very wrong or cruel, some people will certainly turn against him and they may say that he deserves to be treated like that.

Poor Job was getting this kind of treatment without having done a thing to deserve it. But who would believe him? His family and friends had all got the idea into their heads that he must have done something awful. Job describes how he felt: like being walled up in darkness (v.8); like a king stripped of his glory and crown (v.9); like a tree that has been rooted up (v.10), and like being besieged by soldiers in a tent (v.12). Do those things describe how you feel sometimes?

To think over: Jesus bore the kind of treatment that Job endured also. He didn't deserve it.

Prayer: *Dear Lord, make us kind to people in trouble whether they deserve it or not, and may we encourage them to trust You as their Friend. Amen.*

November 23   JOB 28.12–15, 23–28

'Man does not know the way . . . God understands the way . . .' (vs.13,23, RSV).

Comment: Job's mind must have been in a whirl. He had spent days listening to the people around him—his friends, his wife— telling him what they thought he ought to do. How was Job to know the best solution to his problems? He really did want to do the right thing.

Sometimes we are in that kind of situation. There are many

voices giving us their opinions at home, at school, at work, on the television and radio. Where can we find the best advice?

Job came to the right conclusion. 'Behold, the fear of the Lord, that is wisdom' (v.28). God made us and He made the world. Surely the Maker knows best how to direct us.

Question: What is it that makes some people think they know all the answers? Are we in danger of this (1 Corinthians **1.**19; 25)?

Prayer: *Heavenly Father, give us Your wisdom before we pass on advice to others, for Jesus' sake. Amen.*

November 24   **JOB 32.1–10**

'But it is the spirit in a man, the breath of the Almighty, that makes him understand' (v.8, RSV).

Comment: We were particularly worried about one of our children whose job had taken him into a very dangerous part of the world. We believed that God had given him this job to do, but it was hard for us to see him in constant danger. We met a young girl who had been a committed Christian for only a few months, whereas we had been Christians for many years, and she said a wise thing that we have remembered ever since: 'The safest place is in the centre of God's will.' What a wise thing to say from one so young. As verse 9 says, 'It is not the old that are wise, nor the aged that understand what is right'. God's wisdom can come from Christians of any age—even children (Matthew **21.**16).

Elihu had listened to the others politely because they were older and more experienced than he, but they had no answer— just words and words!

Question: Do you think Elihu was right to be angry (v.5)?

Prayer: *Give us Your wisdom and understanding, Lord, so that we can say helpful things to others. Amen.*

November 25   **JOB 38.1–11**

'On what were its bases sunk, or who laid its cornerstone?' (v.6' RSV).

Comment: In recent years we have seen the building and placing of a number of enormous oil rigs in the seas around Great Britain. Divers have to go down and sink the bases and keep a close watch to make sure everything is safe for those working on top. It is too complicated and wonderful for most of us to understand. We accept that they know what they are doing because many lives depend on it.

166

Job had just listened to another long speech which didn't help him to solve anything. At last God silenced all the talking and said a few things Himself. Although Job didn't understand how God had made the universe and kept it going, he knew enough to see that God did it. The universe stayed in place; the stars shone; the tides came in and out to a pattern. Surely Job could trust God to look after him as well.

Think spot: God orders the universe: I can trust Him to order my life.

Prayer: *Teach us how to trust You, Lord God, even though we do not always understand what You are doing. Amen.*

November 26   JOB 42.1–6

'I despise myself' (v.6, RSV).
Comment: Job did not turn his back on God as Satan had hoped, but he had argued a lot and tried to come up with some good reasons for his suffering. It was not until God had spoken and silenced all the arguing that Job realized how rude he had been (40.4, 5; **42**.3).

We sometimes say, 'I wish the floor had opened and swallowed me' when we have made fools of ourselves in front of someone who knows better than we do. Like Job, we don't like ourselves very much as a result.

Job realized that it was not necessary for him to understand why God had acted as He did. He must simply trust Him to do what was best. Job wasn't to know that God had been proving Satan wrong through all that had happened. When we say 'Why doesn't God do something?' in the tragedies around us, we need to remember that He *is* doing something, though we may not understand what it is.

Keynote: Things too wonderful for me, which I did not understand (v.3).
Prayer: *Forgive us when we have thought You didn't care, Lord. We realize that You are always working in the world and in us. Amen.*

November 27   JOB 42.7–9

'You have not spoken of me what is right' (v.8, RSV).
Comment: 'God won't love you if you do that,' one little girl said to another. She must have picked up that wrong idea from someone. It is very important that we should pass on the truth when we tell others about God. Even Job's friends had said, 'You are

suffering as a punishment', which we have seen was far from the truth.

'Cleanliness is next to godliness, as the good Book says' was the favourite text of an old man who lived next door to us. It doesn't come in the Bible at all, but he had believed it to be there for years and years.

Unless we take time to learn the truth about God in the Bible, we may be in danger of misleading others too.

To think over: Just as forgiveness for Job's friends came to them through sacrifice, our forgiveness comes through the death of Jesus.

Prayer: *We pray for those who teach others about You, Lord, that they may know Your truth and pass it on faithfully, for Jesus' sake. Amen.*

November 28   **JOB 42.10–17**

The Lord gave Job twice as much as he had before (v.10, RSV).
Comment: One of the things that many young people dread is the thought of growing old. They think that life will become dull, uninteresting and a burden to them when they can no longer rush around as they do now. But many older people look back and honestly prefer their life now, especially if they are Christians.

Job did not deserve his sufferings any more than he deserved all the good things that God gave him towards the end of his life. All that he had was through the goodness and grace of God, without any 'ifs' and 'buts'.

Health, possessions and family are all very nice to have. Some Christians have them and some do not. But the big lesson that Job learned was that nothing is more important than putting one's life into the personal care of God, for Him to work out His purposes.

Keynote: 'I know that thou canst do all things' (**42.2**).
Prayer: *We thank You for all the good things You allow us to have in life, dear Lord, but we ask that we may not think they are ours by right. We thank You that Your loving care for us is worth more than anything else. Amen.*

It is never easy to speak for God when you know that you will be very unpopular for doing so; and how much more difficult it was going to be for Jeremiah! He was very nearly put to death for telling the people and their leaders what God wanted them to do. But it never pays to hide the truth, and later, when the things which Jeremiah prophesied about actually happened, people knew that he

168

had spoken the truth about God. Christians sometimes have to suffer, too, because they tell the truth. Peter's letter was written to encourage Christians in that position.

November 29   JEREMIAH 1.4–10

'**I chose you before I gave you life, and before you were born I selected you to be a prophet to the nations**' (v.5, GNB).
Comment: It is considered a privilege to read a Bible lesson at our church Family Service but some people, when they are asked to do so are full of excuses! 'I'm nervous!' or 'My voice isn't loud enough' or 'I might not be able to read the hard words properly'. We have to point out that we wouldn't have asked them to read if we hadn't been sure they could do the job.

God chose Jeremiah to be His special messenger to the people but what did he say? Do you make the same excuse?

It doesn't matter if you are eight or eighty, no one is too young, or too old, to tell.
Prayer: *Thank You, Lord, for choosing us as Your followers. Give us the right words to speak for You whenever we have the chance. Amen.*

November 30   JEREMIAH 7.1–7

'**Change the way you are living and stop doing the things you are doing. Be fair in your treatment of one another**' (v.5, GNB).
Comment: We are very fortunate to live in a country where we are free to say what we like, go where we choose, and spend our money how we please, but we need to 'change the way we are living and stop doing the things we are doing' if we want to continue living in a free country.

Most of us have become rather lazy and greedy, we sometimes treat other people unfairly, and do not concern ourselves very much with those less fortunate than ourselves. There may not be many murderers (v.6) in our country, but many worship the false gods of money, possessions and power and do not bother at all about the true God. The warning that Jeremiah gave the Jewish people is one to which we should pay attention.
Prayer: *Lord, show us, as a family, things that we should change and stop doing, and help us all to be fair in our treatment of others, at home, at school, at work, at College, and in our own neighbourhood. Amen.*

You do these things I hate and then you come and stand in my
presence in my own Temple, and say, 'We are safe' (v.10, GNB).
Comment: When you play games do you sometimes choose a
place which you call 'home' or 'den' where you can run to, and
be safe? Some people think of church like that. They think they
can play a game with God all the week, breaking many of His
rules, and then rush into church on Sundays and say, 'We are
safe'.

God isn't impressed with just a weekly attendance at church.
He wants us to say we are sorry for the wrong things in our
lives and then make a determined effort with His help to change
for the better.
Action spot: Could you make up a chorus using the words of
verse 5?
Prayer: *Lord, help us to live the way You want us to at all times
and to know Your presence with us every day and not just on
Sundays, when we go to church. Amen.*

'You are in my hands just like clay in the potter's hands' (v.6,
GNB).
Comment: Once, as I watched a potter at work, I asked him what
happened when a pot 'went wrong'. He pulled a face and showed
me some roughly squeezed balls of clay on a shelf by his wheel.
He told me that they had to be re-kneaded to get all the air
bubbles out and then he would use them again.

When our lives 'go wrong' our Master Potter may need to
squeeze and re-knead us before we can be made into the pleasing
and useful shape for which He has designed us. The squeezing
and re-kneading sometimes hurts, but it is necessary if we are
going to be any good to God. This was the lesson that Jeremiah
had to learn at the potter's house.
Prayer: *Help us to understand Lord, that every experience of life
is designed to teach us something so that we will become the kind
of people that You want us to be. Amen.*

I will put my law within them and write it on their hearts (v.33,
GNB).
Comment: If you have a dog I expect you will be taking him for

a walk some time today. A dog can be taken for two different kinds of walk. Sometimes he is just trailed round the block on a lead because it's a family rule that he has to be exercised every day. At other times, when the sun is shining and everyone is keen to go out, he has a really good run.

In the Old Testament (before Jesus came) people tried to live good lives by keeping a long list of rules. But Jesus made a new covenant (or agreement) with His people so that they would want to do the right thing, and it would no longer be a case of just keeping rules.

Talking point: Talk about things that you do because you have to do them and things you do because you want to. Why is there a difference?

Prayer: *Lord Jesus, so often we try to obey You simply out of a sense of duty. Help us instead to want to please You because of our love for You. We ask this in Your name. Amen.*

December 4   **JEREMIAH 38.1–6**

'By talking like this he is making the soldiers in the city lose their courage' (v.4, GNB).

Comment: 'I'm afraid it can't be mended.'

'This will hurt a little.'

'Your writing is very untidy!'

'You are not quite good enough for the job.'

Do you like to hear the truth, or would you rather not?

Jeremiah told the people, 'God says "If you stay in the city you will die",' but the officials did not want to hear the truth so to stop Jeremiah talking, they put him into a deep muddy pit.

Jesus said: 'Whoever believes in the Son has eternal life; whoever disobeys the Son will not have life but will remain under God's punishment' (John 3.36).

Some people prefer not to be told this truth.

Prayer: *Father, we pray today for those people who do not want to listen to the truths in the Bible but prefer to go their own way. We especially pray for ... Please give them faith to believe and trust in You. Amen.*

December 5   **JEREMIAH 38.7–17**

Then they drew Jeremiah up with ropes and lifted him out (v.13, RSV).

Comment: When you read about rescue operations—freeing trapped miners from a pit-shaft, or people in pot-holing accidents

171

—don't you notice that it is the *rescuer* who does all the work? Jeremiah would certainly have died if Ebed-melech had not decided to rescue him himself, and then done everything that was necessary. He even took rags to bind the ropes so that they would not hurt Jeremiah and cause him any *more* suffering. The poor man was too tired, having been without air, light, food and water, to do anything but allow his weak, helpless body to be drawn up to safety and sunlight. What a wonderful 'picture' this is of what the Lord Jesus did when He came to live in our world, and then die for us on the cross. He did something for us which *we were helpless to do for ourselves*. He lifted us out of the pit of sin. His rescue is so complete that we don't need to suffer any more. All we do is to rely entirely on what *Jesus* has done, and be thankful.

Prayer: *Dear Lord, thank You for coming into this world to save us from sin; and for rescuing us from any more suffering because of it. Amen.*

December 6   1 PETER 1.3–8

Be truly glad! There is wonderful joy ahead, even though the going is rough for a while down here (v.6, Living Bible).

Comment: You may think you get it rough. But what about these Christians. Look at verse 1, and see what had happened to them. Driven out of their homes, out of their jobs, out of the town where they'd always belonged; driven away to live in a strange country where they'd find it hard to get work. There was no dole, no health service, no council houses. Peter wrote a letter to them. He didn't say he felt sorry for them. He said they should be truly glad. Was he crazy? How can we be truly glad when things all around us are going wrong?

To think about: Look at verse 4 and ask God to open your eyes to the real things.

Prayer: *Please help us to understand about the wonderful joy ahead dear Lord. Please give us eyes to see the kind of joy that cannot be touched by illness or war or cruelty or bad temper. Help us to learn how to be truly glad, whatever happens. Amen.*

December 7   1 PETER 1.13–21

So now you can look forward soberly and intelligently to more of God's kindness to you when Jesus Christ returns (v.13, Living Bible).

Comment: Are you looking forward to Christmas? Some people are already looking forward to next year's holiday. Looking forward to things is one of the best joys in life. Looking forward to a treat can give you as much fun as the treat itself.

God has promised us that we can look forward to the return of Jesus Christ. Jesus Himself will really come back to this earth. What a joy for the people who love Him. If a father has to be away from home for a year, everybody misses him. They look forward to his return, and keep themselves cheerful by thinking about the day when he will come. Suppose he came home suddenly and surprised them all by an early return? That's how Jesus will come—suddenly.

Question: Are you looking forward to His return?

Prayer: *Lord Jesus, we are looking forward to You coming back again. May we be ready so that Your coming will not take us by surprise. Amen.*

December 8   **1 PETER 2.1–5**

And now you have become living building-stones for God's use in building his house (v.5, Living Bible).

Comment: What shape are you? Tall and thin, like a pillar? Or short and square and red like a brick? Or round and roly-poly like a cannon ball? Or bent over like an archway? Or are you just an awkward shape—all sharp corners and rough edges? Many of us feel that we are an awkward shape. We just don't seem to fit in with the rest of the family. We don't ever seem to belong to the gang at school. We don't get asked to those parties. We're not the manager's bright boy at work.

Maybe we are awkward, sharp, quarrelsome, proud, unfriendly. Perhaps we need the corners knocked off, and the rough edges smoothed over.

To think about: That's what God can do. He can take awkward people like us and make us exactly the right shape to fit into the building He has planned. We shall see what kind of a building that is tomorrow.

Prayer: *Lord God, a lot needs changing in our lives before we are what You want us to be. Make us the right shape by Your power. Amen.*

December 9   **1 PETER 2.12–17**

It is God's will that your good lives should silence those who foolishly condemn the Gospel without knowing what it can do for them (v.15, Living Bible).

Comment: Do you know what a church is? You may think that is a silly question: a church is that old-fashioned building down the road. No! The Bible says nothing about the church being a stone building down the road. The Bible tells us that God's Church is a group of living people, who fit together and work together. The building that God has planned is made of human hearts, human hands, human brains—all working and planning and loving and praying together.

Where is the Church? It is not just down the road. The Church is everywhere—at home and school, at work, in the shops, in the hospital and wherever Christians live the sort of lives that act out the truth of the gospel.

Prayer: *Help me to be a living part of Your Church today, Lord. Amen.*

December 10   1 PETER 2.18-21

Servants, you must respect your masters and do whatever they tell you (v.18, Living Bible).

Comment: To 'respect' someone means to give them honour and consideration. This is easy when we like those who are over us, but it is not so easy when we don't. We tend to work well for people we like, but our text goes on to say that we must not be so choosy. We must not only obey if our master is kind and reasonable, but equally if he is tough and cruel.

There is no doubt about it that this is not acceptable to most people these days. The Christian way is very hard to follow. That is why Christians can expect suffering. 'This suffering is all part of the work God has given you,' says Peter, the writer (v.21), so no one can say that God hasn't given them anything to do for Him.

Remember: Jesus is not asking us to do anything that He didn't do Himself (v.21). We can be sure that He will look after us.

Prayer: *Father God, we want to please You by following Jesus even though we have to suffer. Please look after us. Amen.*

December 11   1 PETER 2.22-25

He did not threaten to get even (v.23, Living Bible).

Comment: When we have been treated badly by someone and are deeply hurt inside, we are in danger of wanting to get even with the person who has harmed us. If we have done wrong and deserve to be badly treated, it is hard enough, but when we haven't done a thing to deserve it, it is very very difficult to bear.

The Bible tells us that Christians should behave differently from others in situations like these. It can be done. 'Christ, who suffered for you, is your example. Follow in his steps.' Jesus was treated unfairly many times but He never tried to get His own back. He 'left his case in the hands of God who always judges fairly' (v.23). That is what we must do. We can never see the whole reason for people behaving as they do, and we are far from perfect ourselves, so we cannot be trusted to sort things out fairly. God sees the whole picture—them and us—and He will deal with the problems for us.

Think: Jesus never told a lie; never answered back; did not threaten to get even (v.23).

Prayer: *What is impossible to us is possible to You, Lord. Please help us. Amen.*

December 12 **1 PETER 3.8–12**

Instead, pray for God's help for them (v.9, Living Bible).

Comment: A Christian lady was going through a hard time in her church because another Christian was jealous and unkind to her. 'You should be like one big happy family,' says verse 8, but it doesn't always work out that way in our churches and homes, does it?

The Christian lady said, 'It's easy to see faults in others and feel sorry for ourselves, but we ought to remember that the jealous unkind person is unhappy too, and that God has got something better for both of us.' If we realize that, it helps us to pray for God's strength for the one who wrongs us as well as for ourselves.

'Keep control of your tongue' (v.10) is something that many of us are very bad at. We can use that tongue for good right in the middle of the bad if we use it to pray.

To think about: 'The Lord is watching his children, listening to their prayers' (v.12).

Prayer: *Help us to use our tongues to talk to You more often, Lord, and then we shall be less likely to lose control of what we say. Amen.*

December 13 **1 PETER 3.13–17**

Quietly trust yourself to Christ your Lord (v.15, Living Bible).

Comment: 'I don't trust you,' said Jill when Ben held out his fists and asked her to choose which hand it was in. Jill knew what Ben was like because once before he had opened his fist and passed on a spider. She could never be sure of him.

We trust people when we are sure of them. We know Mum and Dad well enough to trust them. They may have to get cross with us sometimes, but we know that they never stop loving us and wanting the best for us.

God wants us to trust Him like that. We can rely on Him not to let us down and He will never stop loving us even though He will have to correct us from time to time.

Think spot: If anyone asks you why you believe in your parents, I am sure you could tell them. Could you tell them why you believe in Jesus (v.15)?

Prayer: *Lord Jesus, we believe You to be completely trustworthy. Help us to live as though we do. Amen.*

December 14   1 PETER 5.1–5

Serve each other with humble spirits (v.5, Living Bible).

Comment: What kind of things cause trouble in your family? Is it when someone behaves selfishly without considering the others? Maybe someone disappears when the washing up needs doing; or goes out without saying where and for how long; or makes plans without consulting the rest of the family. We cannot serve one another when we are all intent on doing our own thing.

A 'humble spirit' means realizing that others are just as important as we are. The amazing thing is that as soon as we begin to treat them as if they are, we are much happier ourselves. 'God gives special blessings to those who are humble' (v.5).

Think spot: The best way to get a humble spirit is to see ourselves as God sees us (v.6). This will make us more thoughtful and helpful to others.

Prayer: *We are sorry for the times when we have thought too highly of ourselves, Lord God. We realize how You must see us. Forgive us for putting ourselves first when we ought to consider others. Amen.*

December 15   1 PETER 5.6–11

'He personally will come and pick you up, and set you firmly in place, and make you stronger than ever' (v.10, Living Bible).

Comment: Our son was in hospital for two weeks for an operation which made him very weak. The day came when we were able to fetch him out. We went to pick him up personally and bring him home, and soon, because his trouble had been put right, he became stronger than ever. The suffering and separation from us was all worth it in the end.

Christians do have to go through trials here on earth, but a day is coming when Jesus will come and collect them personally and take them home to heaven. All the old problems and failures will be over and their faith will be stronger than ever.

Keynote: 'God . . . will give you His eternal glory' (v.10).

Prayer: *We look forward to the time when You will come back again to pick us up, Lord Jesus. Give us strength and patience until that day, and in the meantime, help us to enjoy belonging to You here on earth. Amen.*

December 16   PSALM 103.1–5

Praise the Lord, my soul, and do not forget how kind he is (v.2, GNB).

Comment: Only nine days to Christmas and so many things to be remembered. There are cards to be posted, last-minute presents to be bought and wrapped and food to be laid in for the holiday. Perhaps you have made a list to help you not to forget any of the jobs.

It's easy to remember all the preparations for Christmas and yet forget the Person whom Christmas is all about. Every day—not just at Christmas—God showers us with His presents, and the psalmist goes on to mention some of God's good gifts to us. It might jog our memories if we made a list of some of the things mentioned: sins forgiven, illness healed and life itself are all given to us by God. Present-giving should always be followed by saying thank you to the person who has made the gift. Praising God is the way to say thank You to Him for all that He has done for us.

Think Spot: Think together of some of God's gifts to *your* family during 1978.

Prayer: *Father, we thank You for Your goodness to us and we praise You with all our might. Thank You most of all for the gift of Jesus Christ at Christmas. Amen.*

December 17   PSALM 103.6–18

But for those who honour the Lord, his love lasts for ever (v.17, GNB).

Comment: Crash! The china shepherdess fell from the mantelpiece and smashed into a thousand pieces on the tiled fireplace below. Mum heard the noise and rushed in to see four-year-old Trevor standing nearby looking guilty. 'You naughty boy! I told you never to go near the fire, and now you've broken my favourite ornament.' Trevor let out a howl even before Mum reached him.

When big sister Tina tried to cheer him up he wailed, 'Mum doesn't love me any more', but Mum soon told him that she did.

Good parents never stop loving their children, even though they sometimes have to be cross with them. The psalm writer compares God to the very best kind of father who never stops loving us even when we are bad. But because He loves us, God wants the best for us. He knows that we will be truly happy only when we obey His laws.

To think about: God's children are to 'honour' Him. Talk about what this word means and discuss how, as a family, we may honour God.

Prayer: *Father, on this Your day, may our words and actions bring other people to understand Your greatness and Your love for them. Amen.*

December 18   ISAIAH 1.10,11,15–20

'When you lift your hands in prayer, I will not look at you. No matter how much you pray, I will not listen' (v.15, GNB).

Comment: Sometimes Dad may be too busy watching the football results to answer David's questions, or Mum too intent on her shopping list to listen to Robert's record player. But God is not like that. He is never too busy to listen to His children.

The people of Israel thought they were *very* religious, because they said their prayers and went to church regularly. But God looked right into their hearts. He saw that whatever they might say with their lips, they did not love Him in their hearts or want to obey Him. They may have looked all right in church but the rest of the time they were cheating and lying and ill-treating the weak and poor. So God would not listen to them.

Question: Do we pray and go to church out of habit, or because we love God and want to obey Him? Are we different people on a Monday from on a Sunday?

Prayer: *Lord, make us sincere in all we say to You and all we do in Your name. May our lives match what we say we believe. Help us to 'stop doing evil and learn to do right'. Hear our prayer for Jesus' sake. Amen.*

December 19   ISAIAH 5.1–7

For the vineyard of the Lord of hosts is the house of Israel (v.7, RSV).

Comment: The people of Israel had special festivals, just as we do at Christmas, and one of these was at the finish of the grape harvest. There would be singing and dancing and feasting. Isaiah wanted so much to make the people listen to what God was saying that he went along too. He took his harp—rather like a guitar—and sang a folk song which he had written himself. Everyone enjoyed listening and probably clapped or danced to the rhythm. It seemed to be a song about a disappointing grape harvest, where instead of clusters of rich, large grapes there were only stunted, sour, wild ones for the owner to pick.

But like some pop songs today, Isaiah's song had a message. He meant the fun-loving Israelites to stop and think. They themselves were like the poor harvest. They had failed God, in spite of all His goodness. Isaiah had to warn them that God must punish their sin.

Notice: God looked for good grapes—see verse 7. He wants to see goodness and righteousness in our family too.

Prayer: *Lord, keep us this day from any unjust or evil actions, for Your sake. Amen.*

December 20   **ISAIAH 6.1–8**

'Holy, holy, holy! The Lord Almighty is holy! His glory fills the world' (v.3, GNB).

Comment: Do you ever wonder what God looks like? We can't begin to imagine, because He is so different from us. Isaiah saw a vision of God, but it wasn't what God looked like that impressed him as much as the kind of person God is. God is holy and the word 'holy' means 'set apart'. God is set apart from human beings not just because He is so great and powerful, but because there is no wrong or evil in Him.

Isaiah had only to see God's holiness to realize his own sinfulness and that he was unfit to be near God. Jesus was holy and different from any other person who has lived because His life was quite unspoilt by sin. Yet He came to earth for the very purpose of getting rid of our sin so that we could be made holy too.

Thought: Isaiah had only a vision to show him what God is like. In Jesus we see God face to face (John 14.9).

Prayer: *Lord Jesus, at this Christmas season we remember that You were called Immanuel, which means 'God with us'. Thank You for coming down to earth so that we may know God. Amen.*

179

The people who walked in darkness have seen a great light (v.2, RSV).

Comment: I wonder who arrives home first during term time. Perhaps one of the children is back from school before Mum leaves work. The first thing we do in winter is to switch on the lights, and how different that makes it for those who arrive later! A light gives welcome, cheers and brightens as well as showing the way and making it safe.

Many hundreds of years before Jesus was born, Isaiah had a glimpse of what His coming would be like, not just for Jews but for all the other nations who did not know God. The nearest he can get to describing the joy and cheer of Jesus' birth is to compare it to sudden light flooding the darkness. When we switch on the lights of the Christmas tree, let's remember the light that came into our world with the birth of Jesus.

Thought: Jesus taught His followers that they were to be lights too. Jesus wants our family to shine for Him in the road where we live.

Prayer: *Thank You, Lord, for coming to our dark world to be its light. Make us bright and happy with Your presence and help us to cheer others too. Amen.*

The wolf shall dwell with the lamb, and the leopard shall lie down with the kid (v.6, RSV).

Comment: Dogs and cats sometimes learn to get on together in a family, but we once owned a cat and also a little wild rabbit which we had reared on a bottle, and we were never able to leave them together. The cat waited its chance to catch and kill the rabbit, not because it was a bad cat, but because it was his nature to do so. Wouldn't it be nice if all animals were friends, as Isaiah pictures them?

Yet human beings often act in the same way as animals. Every family knows how children and parents can shout, quarrel and hurt one another. When Adam and Eve first disobeyed God, all nature was spoiled—plants and animals as well as humans. But Isaiah looks far ahead to a wonderful day when everything will be set to rights and no one will hurt or injure any other person. At Jesus' first coming the angels sang 'Peace on earth'. One day we shall see that peace throughout the world.

Question: Does the Prince of Peace bring peace in our family now?

Prayer: *Give peace in our hearts today, Lord, and keep us from hurting or harming others. Amen.*

December 23   ISAIAH 35.3–10

They will be happy for ever, for ever free from sorrow and grief (v.10 GNB).
Comment: Did those verses about the blind, deaf, dumb and lame, remind you of the stories we read about Jesus in the Gospels? When Jesus healed He showed that the wonderful times that Isaiah had foretold were beginning to come true. Many hundreds of years have gone by since Jesus lived on earth and we still see suffering and sadness. Yet we can be happy this Christmas as we remember that when He was born Jesus began the new age of which Isaiah wrote. By His death and resurrection Jesus won the battle against sin, and suffering.

One day the picture will be complete. The very last book of the Bible tells us about a place where there will be no more sighing or sorrow or pain; a place we call heaven where those who love Jesus will be with Him in joy and gladness for ever.
Thought: We can make our home a place of happiness today, if Jesus is with us to help.
Prayer: *Dear Lord Jesus, You cared for the sick and the sad when You were on earth. Please be near to all who are ill or lonely this Christmas time, and show us how we can bring them Your joy. Amen.*

December 24   MATTHEW 1.18–25

And Joseph named him Jesus (v.25, GNB).
Comment: The Jacksons can't decide what to call their new baby. Should he be David like his father, or Harold after his grandfather? Mrs Jackson would like him to be Richard, but older sister Amanda has set her heart on Jonathan.

When Jesus was born, Joseph and Mary had no such trouble deciding on a name, for God had chosen it for them and sent a special message to Joseph beforehand to say what it was to be. Perhaps you think it surprising that God should be concerned about a name, but in those days people took great notice of the *meaning* behind the name. We don't often think about that today. Jesus means 'Saviour' and is a variation of the name Joshua that we find in the Old Testament. Joshua had saved Israel by leading them in battle against their enemies, the people of Canaan, and bringing them into their promised land. Jesus came to save all mankind from a far greater enemy—sin, and to lead them into eternal life with Him in heaven.

Remember: To give thanks, on this Christmas Sunday, for the coming of the Saviour.

Prayer: *Lord, we confess that we are sinful and unable to save ourselves. Thank You for coming to save us from our sins. May many people accept Your salvation this Christmas. Amen.*

Christmas Day   MATTHEW 2.1–12

They knelt down and worshipped him (v.11, GNB).

Comment: Jan's bedroom walls are covered with pictures of her favourite pop group, while Phil's room is decorated with photos and favours of the first division football team he supports. Phil goes to every home match and even travels to some of the away fixtures. When Jan says the players are his idols, he retorts that *she* worships the lead guitar. The word 'worship' was originally 'worth-ship'. It means recognizing the great worth of someone and giving him the love and admiration he deserves. Some people worship other human beings for their skill, money, position or good looks, but the Bible tells us that only one Person deserves and should have our worship, and that is God Himself.

It seems incredible to picture these clever, rich men bowing low before a small baby and giving Him their most valued possessions. Yet they were right to recognize Him as so much more important than they were, for in the cradle lay the King of kings and Son of God.

Thought: Worship leads to the giving of our love, praise, time and belongings.

Prayer: *We worship You this Christmas morning, Lord Jesus. Please take the gifts we offer—our home and our hearts. Amen.*

December 26   MATTHEW 2.13–18

'Herod will be looking for the child in order to kill him' (v.13, GNB).

Comment: There could not be a greater difference between the Wise Men's attitude to Jesus and that of Herod. It has always been true that although most people love someone who is good, others hate and want to get rid of them. Herod was the first to plot the death of Jesus, but all through His life Jesus was hated by those who were vain, greedy and selfish, until envious Jews had Him put to death on the cross.

Boxing Day is also St Stephen's day, when we remember the

first person to be killed for being a Christian (Acts 7). All down the years since then, men and women and young people have been ill-treated because of their goodness and their loyalty to Jesus Christ. While we are still enjoying the happiness of Christmas, let's think of people in countries where to be a Christian means to be in trouble.

Thought: God was in control—*not* king Herod—and He still is.
Prayer: *Thank You, Lord Jesus, for suffering and dying for us. Please be close today to those who suffer for Your sake. May they know that You are in control. Make us brave enough to let others know that we love and serve You. Amen.*

December 27   **MATTHEW 2.19–23**

He ... came to live in a small town called Nazareth (v.23, J. B. Phillips).
Comment: *I'd* like to live near a big city where there's plenty going on, but other people would prefer a cottage in the country or a house by the sea. We often feel that we could be happier or more successful if only we lived somewhere else.

The Lord Jesus Christ could have chosen the very best and smartest place to live, but it's a comfort to find that He grew up instead in a rather scruffy small town. No one thought much of Nazareth or expected any one who had been brought up there to make good. Jesus certainly didn't mix with the 'best' people or go to the best schools. He learned to get on with ordinary folk in a humdrum place. But what really mattered was that He had a loving home and parents who cared for Him, and who taught their children to trust in God and love the Scriptures.

Thought: The atmosphere of our home is what matters most, not the size of the house or where we live.
Prayer: *Lord, help us to make our home a centre of love and warmth towards others and a place where You are honoured and obeyed. Amen.*

December 28   **2 JOHN 1–6**

And this is love, that we follow his commandments (v.6, RSV).
Comment: The Beatles used to sing, 'Love is all you need' and St Augustine said, 'Love God and do what you like'. The apostle John puts the same stress on love. He explains what the Bible means by love. Love, John says, always leads us to obey. When we are really fond of someone, we want to do the things that

183

please them rather than follow our own wishes. This is even more true where love for God is concerned.

Perhaps John was remembering what Jesus, his Master, said on the evening before He died. He told the disciples, 'If you love me you will keep my commandments' (John 14.15). In the Gospels we can find many instructions that Jesus gave for those who wished to follow Him. If we want to show our love for Jesus we shall try, with His help, to put them into practice.

Question: What commands of Jesus should we, as a family, be obeying?

Prayer: *Lord, on the days when we find it difficult to feel love for You, help us to show it just the same by our obedience. Amen.*

December 29   **2 JOHN 7–13**

Anyone who does not stay with the teaching of Christ, but goes beyond it, does not have God (v.9, GNB).

Comment: Some people think that the 'dear Lady' to whom John writes is not a mother with her family, but the little group of Christians who formed the church in that place. At that time there were many wandering preachers who travelled round visiting and teaching. Some were good and true, but others were bad and false. All would require food and a bed for the night during their stay, but John is anxious that the little church should welcome *only* those who taught the truth about Jesus and the Christian way of life.

So he warns his readers *always* to compare what the visitors say with the teaching of Jesus Christ Himself, and never to welcome those who contradicted or added to that teaching. This rule would save them from being led into believing lies.

Note: Those first readers had no New Testament to read as we have. We can test the truth of what we believe and what others teach by what the Bible says.

Prayer: *Thank You, Lord, for Your Word the Bible. Help us to read and study it so that we may learn the truth and our faith may never be shaken. Amen.*

December 30   **3 JOHN 1–8**

You are doing a fine faithful piece of work, dear friend, in looking after the brothers who come your way, especially when you have never seen them before (v.5, J. B. Phillips).

Comment: 'Don't forget I've asked that visiting missionary to come to tea tomorrow,' Mum said on Saturday night. 'Well *I* shan't come in—I'll have my tea in the kitchen,' Keith said. 'It's not much fun having someone we don't even know,' Sue complained. 'Shall I be expected to help?' Mum sighed. Perhaps she shouldn't have invited him, but he seemed to have nowhere else to go.

John gives a special word of praise and gratitude for this Christian called Gaius, who was entertaining visiting preachers, even though they were strangers to him. John saw it as a special work for God. It's also something that all the family can share in, because 'looking after' a visitor means seeing that they feel comfortable and welcome in every kind of way.

To think about: Discuss how the whole family can take a share in looking after visitors, as a work for God.

Prayer: *Lord Jesus, when we have Christians or anyone into our home, help us to behave as if we were having You to tea and to give our best in every way. For Your sake. Amen.*

December 31   **3 JOHN 9–15**

Peace be with you (v.15, GNB).

Comment: If you have met any modern day Israelis you will know that they still use the age-old Jewish greeting 'Shalom' or 'Peace'. Perhaps they do not always think of the meaning any more than we remember that 'Good-bye' really means 'God be with you'. When John used the familiar greeting to Gaius, he may have recalled how Jesus Himself gave the greeting of 'Peace be with you' to His disciples after His resurrection (John 20.19).

As the old year ends, we all need the peace that Jesus gives. He wants to give us peace about the past. He does not mean us to drag the guilt, failures and sorrows of the old year into the new. He can give peace in our family too. His peace means more than stopping fights and quarrels, for Jesus wants us to have healthy, whole relationships with one another with old scores forgotten and grudges forgiven.

Thought: God wants to give us peace about the future as well as the past, whatever our family problems might be.

Prayer: *Lord, we confess the sins and failures of 1978. Give us the peace of Your forgiveness. As we face the new and unknown year, give us the peace that comes from knowing that You are in control and that You are with our family always. Amen.*

Bible
Reading

For the family . .

All Publications available
from your
local Christian bookshop
or from
Scripture Union (Mail Order)
P.O. Box 38
BRISTOL BS99 7NA

For the under 7's

Simon and Sarah

Bible truths are presented
in a way which young members
of the family will understand and enjoy.

Six-year-old Simon,
and Sarah, who is five,
discover many new and exciting
things about God through
their everyday lives and experiences.
The series of twelve books
may be started at any point,
as each book is a separate
unit, containing thirty days'
material.

*Fully illustrated with things to do
and pictures to colour.*

For the 7–8's

Stepping Stones

Stepping Stones are 12 books,
designed for the boy or girl who has
completed the 'Simon and Sarah'
books but is not yet ready for 'Quest'.

This series takes the major stories
and characters of the Bible and
shows vividly how they apply to the
life experiences of boys and girls
today.

They are fully illustrated and
contain a complete range of puzzles,
quizzes and other activity materials.

A New look for ..

quest *8–11's*

Covers carefully selected parts of the
Bible over a two-year period.
   Pictures, puzzles, questions to answer
. . . all help to aid understanding of the
Bible readings.

key notes *11–14's*

Interesting and lively comment on a large
part of the Bible over a four-year period.
The series gives many opportunities for
personal discovery and practical
application.

As from 1979 both these publications will
take on a new, larger format, making it
possible to present the notes in a more
imaginative and lively way.
Quest and Key Notes will continue to be
dated and published quarterly.

For older teens and adults..

LIVING TRUTH

Four paperbacks for new Christians who want to come to grips with the teaching of the New Testament.

A popular style and a popular version (Living Bible) lead the reader into a developing awareness of God's message for today. Cartoon illustrations give the series an instant-tell appeal.

LOVING THE JESUS WAY
GOING THE JESUS WAY
LIVING THE JESUS WAY
GROWING THE JESUS WAY